T0299436

TEACHING MACROECONOMICS
WITH MICROSOFT EXCEL®

Humberto Barreto strives to deliver fundamental content for an undergraduate macroeconomics course via Microsoft Excel® that any economist can easily use in the classroom. His contribution is to provide a complement to conventional teaching that gives professors a different way to present macro models and incorporate data into their courses. The Excel files are meant for students, while the audience for this book is professors.

The Excel workbooks and add-ins available on the Web at www.depauw .edu/learn/macroexcel are designed to be used by students with any textbook. Each Excel workbook contains links to screencasts: recordings of the computer screen, also known as a video screen capture, with audio narration. Each screencast is short, approximately five to ten minutes in duration, and walks the student through the steps needed to complete a task.

Humberto Barreto is Elizabeth P. Allen Distinguished University Professor at DePauw University, Greencastle, Indiana. Born in Camagüey, Cuba, Dr Barreto earned his PhD from the University of North Carolina at Chapel Hill. He is co-author (with Frank M. Howland) of *Introductory Econometrics Using Monte Carlo Simulation with Microsoft Excel®* and author of *Intermediate Microeconomics with Microsoft Excel®*. Dr Barreto has been a Fulbright Scholar in the Dominican Republic, has won several teaching awards, and has given workshops all over the world on how to improve the teaching of economics and econometrics. He has also written several articles on pedagogical applications of Excel®.

TEACHING MACROECONOMICS WITH MICROSOFT EXCEL®

HUMBERTO BARRETO
DePauw University, Greencastle, Indiana

CAMBRIDGE
UNIVERSITY PRESS

CAMBRIDGE
UNIVERSITY PRESS

Shaftesbury Road, Cambridge CB2 8EA, United Kingdom

One Liberty Plaza, 20th Floor, New York, NY 10006, USA

477 Williamstown Road, Port Melbourne, VIC 3207, Australia

314–321, 3rd Floor, Plot 3, Splendor Forum, Jasola District Centre, New Delhi – 110025, India

103 Penang Road, #05–06/07, Visioncrest Commercial, Singapore 238467

Cambridge University Press is part of Cambridge University Press & Assessment, a department of the University of Cambridge.

We share the University's mission to contribute to society through the pursuit of education, learning and research at the highest international levels of excellence.

www.cambridge.org
Information on this title: www.cambridge.org/9781107584983

© Humberto Barreto 2016

This publication is in copyright. Subject to statutory exception and to the provisions of relevant collective licensing agreements, no reproduction of any part may take place without the written permission of Cambridge University Press & Assessment.

First published 2016

A catalogue record for this publication is available from the British Library

Library of Congress Cataloging-in-Publication data
Names: Barreto, Humberto, 1960– author.
Title: Teaching macroeconomics with Microsoft Excel / by Humberto Barreto.
Description: New York, NY : Cambridge University Press, 2016.
Identifiers: LCCN 2015040091 I ISBN 9781107584983 (paperback)
Subjects: LCSH:Macroeconomics – Study and teaching. I Microsoft Excel (Computer file)
Classification: LCC HB172.5 .B359 2016 I DDC 339.0285/554–dc23
LC record available at http://lccn.loc.gov/2015040091

ISBN   978-1-107-58498-3   Paperback

Additional resources for this publication at www.depauw.edu/learn/macroexcel

Cambridge University Press & Assessment has no responsibility for the persistence or accuracy of URLs for external or third-party internet websites referred to in this publication and does not guarantee that any content on such websites is, or will remain, accurate or appropriate.

Para mi familia:

Tami, Tyler, Nicolas, y Jonah

Contents

All files are freely available online at
www.depauw.edu/learn/macroexcel

Preface

My simple idea is to deliver fundamental content in an undergraduate macroeconomics course via Microsoft Excel® in a way that any economist can easily use for teaching purposes. My contribution is to provide a complement to conventional teaching that gives professors a different way to present macro models and incorporate data into their courses. The Excel files are meant for students, whereas the audience for this book is fellow professors.

A series of implications flow from the decision to target this book toward professors:

- A great deal of basic information can be safely omitted.
- Content is modular and stand-alone, so teachers can pick and choose what to use.
- Explanations are less detailed.
- Mathematics is used to present models compactly.
- Successful pedagogical practices or suggestions are included.
- Focus is placed on implementing models in Excel, including modifying the models.
- There is an emphasis on data sources and ways to quickly update data for class presentation.
- The writing style is more conversational because target readers are my peers.

The Excel workbooks and add-ins, available on the Web at www.depauw .edu/learn/macroexcel, are designed to be used by students with any textbook. Each Excel workbook contains links to *screencasts*: recordings of the computer screen, also known as a video screen capture, with audio narration. Each screencast is short, approximately five to ten minutes in duration, and walks the student through the steps needed to complete a task. All videos are grouped in a channel, available at vimeo.com/channels/macroexcel. A complete listing of all screencasts, organized by workbook, is available at www.depauw.edu/learn/macroexcel/screencasts.

This printed book describes each screencast, highlighting important points, as a way to minimize the time needed to choose which ones to use. It is recommended, however, that you view screencasts selected for your students to make sure you are familiar with the material, especially Excel functions and add-ins.

Although primarily designed with a course in intermediate macro in mind, many of the files and screencasts are useful for other courses. *Maddison-Data.xls*, for example, could be used in introductory economics, development, and growth theory courses. *Unem.xls* could serve as a supplement for any labor economics textbook. Because the content is modular, the professor can pick and choose what, when, and how to use a particular Excel file or screencast. For intermediate macro, simply plug workbooks as appropriate into an existing syllabus – there is no need to follow the order in which the files are listed. If your course begins with a review of key macro variables, then it would make sense to jump right into the workbooks that use the FRED Excel add-in to download data.

The innovation and unique contribution of this book and the associated Excel files springs from my ability to recast existing knowledge into Excel, which turns out to have powerful advantages for communicating ideas and displaying data to students. Through using these macro-enhanced workbooks and materials, students will more fully learn sophisticated concepts that are often poorly absorbed through conventional books and lectures.

One powerful advantage of delivering the material to students via Excel is that the files can be easily updated by me or modified by you. Parameters can be quickly changed to create new questions, text can be altered or augmented as needed, and entirely new worksheets can be inserted with new material. If a workbook is used as an in-class lecture, you can simply delete or hide unwanted sheets, such as the *ToDo* sheet (which has video links and a list of tasks for students).

I will keep the Excel workbooks updated, correcting mistakes and adding buttons and other features. I will not update the screencasts as frequently, and they may not look exactly like the latest version of the Excel files. Of course, if major changes are made and the screencast is badly out of date, I will redo it.

I assume my audience (both student and professor) has used Excel but is unfamiliar with advanced Excel functionality and has never opened Visual Basic or written a macro. The workbooks cover a wide range of Excel skills, such as basic and advanced charting (e.g., making a graph with two y axes, adding recession bars to a chart, and creating a population pyramid), pivot tables, conditional formatting, and using *Solver* and other add-ins. All code is open source and can be viewed by pressing ALT-F11 while in Excel with a macro-enhanced workbook open.

I want to thank many people for contributions to this work, including generations of students and many colleagues. They had to listen to me complain about how economists had failed to take advantage of technology to improve their teaching and then put up with many Visual Basic errors and crashes. I thank the many colleagues and students on whom I imposed to read drafts and test drive Excel files. The following helped me by sending me specific comments and suggestions: Sean Brocklebank, Mary Dixon, Bill Goffe, Peter Mikek, Imad Moosa, Kerry Pannell, Alberto Posso, Guangjun Qu, Tikhon Savrasov, George Tawadros, and Dan Wachter. I also benefited from the criticisms and comments of four anonymous reviewers.

In addition, three others deserve special thanks: Frank Howland, Kay Widdows, and Tami Barreto. Frank and I collaborated on an econometrics book that uses Excel, and we worked closely together for many years. A long time ago, he helped me implement and solve the Solow Model in Excel. He does not know this, but when I write something, I think of him reading and criticizing it, which then forces me to make it better. Kay and I team-taught several courses and created a series of Excel-based labs for Principles of Economics. She is neither a macroeconomist nor a programmer but has a sharp eye for clear explanation and organization of ideas. I learned a great deal from both of them, and much of the material in these workbooks and screencasts bears their imprint. Tami copyedited this book and the Excel files, greatly improving the exposition by toning down my colloquial style and pushing for clarity in expression. She has edited just about everything I have ever written, and I am glad to be able to recognize her contribution.

Finally, I thank DePauw University, RMIT, and Cambridge University Press. DePauw's Elizabeth P. Allen Endowed Chair and Allen A. Wilkinson Faculty Fellowship programs provided generous financial and course release support for this project. RMIT provided a supportive environment that helped me work on this book during a productive and enjoyable sabbatical year in Melbourne, Australia. I remain surprised that Cambridge University Press is willing to publish this book. The Press will not make much money, because students do not have to buy this book, and it really is quite weird. Taking a chance on this unorthodox work is a testament to the Press's mission as a publisher of high-quality, innovative material. I deeply thank my editor, Karen Maloney, for all her support.

I welcome all questions, criticisms, and suggestions. I hope my mistakes and deficiencies in exposition do not prevent you from helping your students learn.

Software Requirements and Opening a Macro-Enhanced Workbook

> The idea for the electronic spreadsheet came to me while I
> was a student at the Harvard Business School, working on
> my MBA degree, in the spring of 1978.
> – Dan Bricklin

The materials in this book will work on any Windows Excel version all the way back to 1997 (version 8). The workbooks and add-ins were created and are optimized for use with Windows Excel, but they can be accessed with a Macintosh computer. Microsoft removed Visual Basic from Mac Excel 2008 but reversed that decision in Mac Excel 2011, so this version should work. *Solver* in Mac Excel 2011 remains as temperamental as ever. The best solution for Mac users is to emulate Windows with software such as Parallels or Boot Camp. For on-campus users, accessing Excel from a server (see, e.g., VMWare's Horizon View client) is an easy solution for Mac users. This is my default method for enabling students with Macs and tablets to access the files.

To ensure that older versions of Excel can open these files, workbooks have been saved in "compatibility mode" (Excel 97–2003 Workbook) with the .xls filename extension. In Excel 2007 (version 12) or later, be sure to save the workbooks as .xls files or in the special "excel macro-enabled workbook" format, which carries the .xlsm extension. If you save the workbook as an Excel workbook with the .xlsx extension, the macros will not be saved, and functionality will be lost.

There was a substantial jump from Excel 2003 to Excel 2007. The interface was radically rearranged, with the Ribbon replacing menus and toolbars, while under the hood the charting engine was completely overhauled and the maximum size of a sheet was increased to 1,048,576 (2^{20}) rows by 16,384 (2^{14}) columns. The instructions in the files refer to Excel 2007 and later versions, using the Ribbon. The screencasts were made with Excel 2010 (version 14) and Excel 2013 (version 15), but other versions are similar enough that you can figure out what to do and the files will work on any version based on

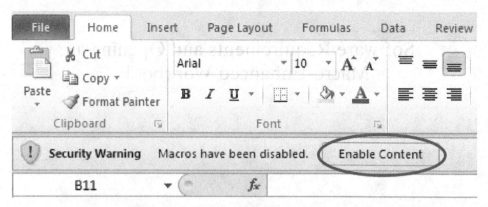

Figure 1. Opening a workbook with macros in Excel 2013.

Visual Basic. (You probably did not notice, but Excel 2007, version 12, was followed by Excel 2013, version 14. It turns out that Microsoft decided to skip version 13 because it is an unlucky number.)

For non-English versions of Excel, the files will work in the sense that buttons, scroll bars, and macros will function; however, the add-ins and other content will not be translated. Fortunately, you can easily add text boxes or other explanatory text in cells, as needed.

Finally, while OpenOffice did not provide much of a challenge, Google Docs caught Microsoft's attention. OneDrive.com and Office365.com offer cloud alternatives to traditional installations of software on your machine. Regrettably, as of this writing, because of security concerns, they do not support Visual Basic, a limitation that renders these options useless for working with these macro-enhanced files from within a Web browser. You can save a file with macros in your favorite storage area in the cloud, but you will need to download and open it with desktop Excel to run the macros. Within a browser, as of this writing, macros cannot be executed.

Accessing and Using the Excel Workbooks

Visit http://www.depauw.edu/learn/macroexcel to download the files that accompany this book. You may download files as needed, to as many different computers or devices as required. For security and efficiency in transmission (some files are quite large and should not be e-mailed), it is best if you send links to screencasts and Excel workbooks to students and colleagues.

Figure 1 shows that, when opening a workbook with macros, Excel will alert you to their presence with a security warning under the Ribbon (and right above the formula bar).

Click *Enable Content* to allow the buttons and other controls in the workbook to function properly. You may also be asked if you want to enable editing on the file – you should accept this offer.

If you do not see the security warning or have no opportunity to enable content, your security level has been set to block all files with macros. Although malicious code can be harmful, you must dial down the safety measures to allow Excel to utilize fully the information in the workbook. Close the file and change the security setting to allow Excel to open files with macros. In Excel 2010 and 2013, open the Excel Options dialog box (execute **File → Options**). Click **Trust Center** and then the **Trust Center Setting** button. In the **Trust Center** dialog box, click **Macro Settings** and select **Disable all macros with notification**. Click **OK** twice to return to Excel and reopen the file, which should now offer the enable content option displayed in Figure 1.

If buttons or other controls do not work, the first thing to check is that you have enabled macros. Another simple fix for many problems is to quit Excel and start over. Visit http://www.depauw.edu/learn/macroexcel to see a list of problems and solutions. Contact me and I will do my best to help you. If you get a Visual Basic error, click **Debug** and carefully note the text in the yellow-highlighted line – this is the where the code crashed and where the search for a fix begins.

The screencast links embedded in the workbooks do not require any special software or other preparation. Simply click on a link and the user's default browser is used to display the video, streamed from Vimeo.com. A complete listing of all screencasts, organized by workbook, is available at http://www.depauw.edu/learn/macroexcel/screencasts. Links can be sent via e-mail or placed on your course web page.

Modifying Visual Basic Code

Although the macros in the workbooks are meant simply to be run by button clicks, they can be viewed and modified. Most users would never have occasion to examine the code, but if you are able to read and write in Visual Basic, all of the macros are open and accessible.

Of course, the code from any button (or other object, such as a scroll bar) can also be accessed via right clicking and editing the assigned macro. It is not expected that a student or professor will need to modify a macro, but the potential is there. Examining the code in these workbooks can be an excellent way to learn Visual Basic.

Sources and Further Reading

For more on the history of the electronic spreadsheet, as told by one of its creators, see http://bricklin.com/visicalc.htm. This is the source for the epigraph.

On Microsoft skipping version 13, see www.neowin.net/news/office-14-slated-for-a-20092010-release: "In December 2006, Eric Vigesaa, Program

Manager for Office system client applications, stated during a TechNet radio chat: '13 is unlucky, so we're calling it Office 14.'"

Visit Office.com to determine your version number, download updates, and more.

I recommend the following websites for Excel tips and tricks, workbook and add-in downloads, and Visual Basic code snippets:

- Ron de Bruin: www.rondebruin.nl
- Charley Kyd: www.exceluser.com
- Tushar Mehta: www.tushar-mehta.com/excel
- Chip Pearson: www.cpearson.com/excel
- Jon Peltier: http://peltiertech.com/Excel
- Andy Pope: www.andypope.info

Introduction: Why Simulation and Excel?

> At this stage of the argument the general public, though
> welcome at the debate, are only eavesdroppers at an
> attempt by an economist to bring to an issue the deep
> divergences of opinion between fellow economists which
> have for the time being almost destroyed the practical
> influence of economic theory, and will, until they are
> resolved, continue to do so.
> – John Maynard Keynes

This book is meant to be read and used by professors and economists. It assumes familiarity with economic theory and data analysis, so it will not make sense to a student or beginner. It is a manual for utilizing teaching materials that are available on the Web at http://www.depauw.edu/learn/ macroexcel. It is assumed that the professor has a favorite textbook or readings that neither this book nor the online files will replace. Instead, delivery of content via Microsoft Excel will supplement and improve the teaching and learning process.

After explaining what is available and how to use it, this introduction presents a pedagogical argument in favor of simulation and Excel. Much of our teaching in economics is based on how we were taught and what we feel works, but advances in neuroscience make clear that many of our strategies and methods are flawed.

Excel Files and Screencasts

Professors who use these materials will have their students work with two types of resources: Excel files and screencasts (video recordings of the computer screen with audio narration). The Excel files include macro-enhanced workbooks that contain everything students need, including a *ToDo* sheet with links to screencasts and tasks (i.e., questions) to enable assessment. In addition, Excel add-ins, special files that extend the functionality of Excel, are provided.

Each chapter in this book lists the workbooks and screencasts available with a brief description providing a quick overview of the content and enabling professors to zero in on appropriate material. Each chapter begins with a section on common student problems and recommendations for ways to minimize confusion. The rest of the chapter is then devoted to more detailed description of the content in the workbooks and screencasts, answers to tasks, and suggestions for teaching.

The pedagogical principle behind the Excel workbooks and screencasts is that of strongly guided instruction via worked examples. The screencasts are meant to be viewed with Excel open so that each step can be replicated. Videos can be paused or repeatedly replayed as often as needed. Some tasks are easy, requiring simple replication, while others do more than simply repeat the screencasts by asking the student to extend a result or consider a related, but different, scenario.

How to Provide Students with Files

The easiest way to deliver a workbook or screencast to students is to send an e-mail with the link. For example, suppose someone is having trouble creating a chart in Excel. Visit the *Teaching Macro with Excel* website at http://www .depauw.edu/learn/macroexcel and go to the *Screencasts* page. Right-click the first screencast and copy the link address (http://vimeo.com/econexcel/ how-to-chart-in-excel). Paste the link into an e-mail and send it. When the student receives the e-mail and clicks on the link, he or she will go directly to the screencast.

This same procedure can be used to send an Excel workbook: right-click any file on the *Excel Workbooks* page of the *Teaching Macro with Excel* web-site, copy the address, and paste it into an e-mail. When the recipient clicks on the link, the workbook will download and open in Excel.

Links to workbooks and screencasts from a course management system (e.g., Moodle or Blackboard) or class web pages are another way to deliver files to students. In addition, Excel workbooks may be downloaded and saved on network drives, in course folders, or to other locations to which students have access. Finally, the link to the website itself, http://www.depauw.edu/ learn/macroexcel, can be shared with students and colleagues.

How to Teach with These Resources

As a professor, you can use these materials in several ways. You can view the videos in a workbook, practice and perfect the tasks on your own, then project the file in class and incorporate it into your lecture. In a lab setting, the entire class could watch a video, after which you could provide personalized support as students work on specific tasks on their own. You can also simply distribute a workbook to your students (via a link in an e-mail or by providing the workbook itself on a network drive) and have them view the screencasts and complete assigned tasks as homework. A truly radical idea would invert the classroom – assign a workbook so that students view and replicate the screencasts as homework, then have them come to class to do the tasks with your help and support. I did this in spring 2014, and I offer handouts, teaching notes, and exams online at http://www.depauw.edu/learn/macroexcel.

The files can be projected in class as part of a lecture, used in lab settings, or assigned as homework, but they do not replace a textbook or professor. The Excel files are meant as complements, not substitutes, to a traditional book, and the professor is responsible for picking and choosing which workbooks to use as supplements as well as when and how to use them. This printed book offers guidance and information to help you make these pedagogical decisions. It has suggestions on how to teach the material and use the files. It also points out where and how students might struggle with concepts or in using Excel.

ToDo **Sheet Task Answers**

Each workbook has a list of questions in a *ToDo* sheet that require students to replicate aspects of a screencast and apply a concept or test a claim. These tasks vary in difficulty and are described in this book.

There is no master answer key to the tasks, but some answers are provided in concealed sheets in the workbooks, which can be revealed by running the *ToggleHideUnhide* macro using any of these three methods: (1) from the **Developer** tab, click **Macros**; (2) press ALT-F8 and select the *ToggleHideUn-hide* macro and click **Run**; or (3) use the keyboard shortcut CTRL-SHIFT-U. These answer sheets cannot be seen simply by viewing the hidden sheets in the workbook because they are given the special property of being *VeryHid-den* and can only be revealed by running the macro. The code, however, is not password protected, so a student expert in Visual Basic could access these sheets. This seems highly unlikely, but if this concerns you, reveal and delete the answer sheets before distributing the workbook. Answers to some tasks, along with tips for easy grading, are described in this book. Sometimes the question is so obvious that no answer is provided.

Why Simulation?

All of the workbooks rely on using Excel to create concrete illustrations and strong visual displays of theoretical concepts. Models and theories are implemented in Excel, and simulation is used to explore and explain properties and behaviors. This is the fundamental advantage of teaching with a spreadsheet. Instead of a dead graph that has been prepared by someone else, Excel enables students to change a parameter and instantly observe its effect on endogenous variables. The ability to control which exogenous variable is manipulated and to see the results on-screen as a shift of or movement along a curve is key to the learning process. The student creates relationships between variables and can literally see theoretical connections that used to require difficult abstract thinking. The student can also perform an endless series of experiments with random parameters, discovering and exploring comparative statics properties.

There is perhaps no better example of the power of simulation and visual presentation than the Solow Model. Its iterative, dynamic operation puts growth theory beyond the grasp of almost all undergraduate students. While a book can certainly show the model's solution in a Solow diagram, once technological progress is added so that the steady state is displayed in terms of efficiency units, it is unreasonable to expect the typical undergraduate to be able to map the solution to a graph of actual output or consumption over time. Excel can do this transformation quickly, with striking graphs that make clear how technological progress is the key to modern economic growth. Changing parameters and answering comparative statics questions enable students to truly understand the model. The easy access to data (population and GDP per capita) to calibrate the model and test theoretical predictions with real-world outcomes is icing on the cake.

In fact, I would argue that simulation should become part of every economist's teaching toolkit. Schmidt (2003) points out that there is a substantial literature on simulations, games, and experiments in the classroom and focuses on computerized simulations. After listing several benefits, Schmidt turns to costs:

The instructor has to be able to install and run the simulation, and someone has to code the simulation.

Once written, however, the code can be easily shared with many different instructors. It would be desirable to have a central database of publically available simulation programs to facilitate sharing them. Schmidt (2003, 154)

Fortunately, because the simulation of the Solow Model is embedded in the Excel workbooks, the installation costs are negligible – simply download and open the workbook (enabling macros) and it is ready to go. As for the central database of simulation programs suggestion, visit "Teaching with Simulations," available at http://serc.carleton.edu/sp/library/simulations, for an overview of simulation pedagogy and example applications.

Grossman (1999, 93) points out tangible advantages of teaching with simulation: "We find that performing queuing simulations in spreadsheets offers six benefits: explicitness, immediacy, insight, flexibility, active modeling, and accessibility. These benefits apply not only to students, but also to instructors with expertise in queuing theory." Each of these benefits has a common root – it reduces abstraction. This is the core, pedagogical trump card of simulation and explains why teaching with spreadsheet implementations of models is so effective.

Why Excel?

Even if one accepts that simulation is a powerful teaching tool, there is still the issue of the appropriate software to use. The choice set is large, from open-source spreadsheets to R to Java applets or other browser-based implementations to high-end mathematical packages such as Matlab and Mathematica. Barreto (2015) makes the case that Excel is "just right," not too easy so that anyone can master it and not too hard so that it does not require large start-up investment.

A moment's reflection should convince you of the latter claim. Students have experience with Excel and are quite comfortable with it. They can add and subtract cells and use formulas to compute sums and averages. You can tell any student to type "= RAND()" in a cell and hit F9, thereby instantly producing a random number generator. There is no programming needed. Of course, in a macro-enhanced workbook, students can click buttons and scroll bars to change variables and immediately see the updated display.

But there is a world of Excel knowledge beyond the rudimentary skills of the typical student. It is in acquiring advanced skills and mastery that Excel proves to be the optimal software choice. Charting provides a good example. Although most students can select data and create a chart, they must be taught how to properly label it, and there are many additional charting features that they can apply (as described in the next chapter). Learning how to use advanced Excel functions, install and manage add-ins, and analyze data demonstrates a level of proficiency that is not easily attained and that employers keenly desire. By learning economics via Excel, the student is also acquiring valuable skills in Excel. The student is aware of this value and is willing to work hard, certainly much harder than in a standard chalk-and-talk course. For the professor interested in maximizing student learning, this may be the best reason of all to use Excel.

Conclusion

You would think that professors know how students learn, but just like everyone else, we hold on to incorrect beliefs, and our intuition can lead us astray. For example, Brown et al. (2014) point out that most people believe cramming is an effective method because it feels like hard work. In fact, interleaved practice and spacing the material is vastly superior to repeating the same thing. Experiments have consistently shown that shooting a basketball from different areas or throwing different pitches is far better than shooting from the exact same place or throwing the exact same pitch for an entire practice.

Similarly, you might think that Excel is a big distraction that necessarily subtracts from economics content. After all, if the brain is a reservoir of fixed size, then Excel crowds out economics. This zero-sum model is completely wrong. When it comes to learning, bombarding the mind with many sensory inputs is much better than a single channel. This is why listening to a lecture passively is inferior to listening and taking notes, which in turn is inferior to working with a computer (with its additional stimuli). The natural sciences take this to another level when students do lab work – now they are actively moving their hands and using all of their senses so that their brains are making all kinds of connections.

The physical processes involved in learning, encoding information so it can be retrieved and used later, is complicated. Medina (2008, 104) says, "The little we know suggests that it is like a blender left running with the lid off. The information is literally sliced into discrete pieces as it enters the brain and splattered all over the insides of our mind." When you look at a graph, your brain performs a series of remarkable steps. Lines are separated from curves and stored in different areas of the brain. Colors, numbers, sound, motion, and other information of what we see, hear, feel, smell, and taste are distributed all throughout the brain. What neuroscientists call the binding problem, that is, how the brain manages and reconstructs all of these bits of data, is the focus of intense research.

With this model of the brain, it makes sense that multiple inputs entrench information more deeply and give more hooks for retrieval. A lecture on the Solow Model with a homework assignment one day that is followed by a screencast and in-class problem session and then a computer-lab meeting is better than three lectures on the same material. We exclusively lecture because it is low cost, not because it maximizes learning.

Augmenting your classroom with Excel (and other ways of delivering content) is sure to improve your teaching and how much your students learn. This book gives you the opportunity to incorporate Excel into your curriculum with little effort. The material is modular, so you can pick and choose what to use. You can also vary how you utilize the files, from displaying them in a lecture to assigning them as homework or working together in a computer lab to flipping the classroom. Experimentation and change are the keys to successful teaching. This book offers a low-cost way to try out new ways to teach economics.

Sources and Further Reading

The epigraph is from the preface to J. M. Keynes, *The General Theory of Employment, Interest and Money* (1936), http://www.marxists.org/reference/subject/economics/keynes/general-theory.

On simulation as a teaching tool:

Grossman, T. 1999. "Teachers' Forum: Spreadsheet Modeling and Simulation Improves Understanding of Queues." *Interfaces* 29, no. 3: 88–103.

Schmidt, S. 2003. "Active and Cooperative Learning Using Web-Based Simulations." *Journal of Economic Education* 34, no. 2: 151–67.

For a review of spreadsheets in the teaching of economics and a detailed argument in favor of Excel:

Barreto, H. 2015. "Why Excel?" *Journal of Economic Education* 46, no. 3: 300–309. http://www.tandfonline.com/doi/abs/10.1080/00220485.2015.1029177.

The lessons of modern neuroscience with respect to learning make for interesting and helpful reading for professors and advisers:

Brown, Peter C., Henry L. Roediger, and Mark A. McDaniel. 2014. *Make It Stick: The Science of Successful Learning.* Belknap Press of Harvard University Press.

Medina, John M. 2008. *Brain Rules: 12 Principles for Surviving and Thriving at Work, Home and School.* Pear Press.

1
Charting in Excel

1.1

Introduction

[With a chart,] as much information may be *obtained in five minutes as would require whole days to imprint on the memory in a lasting manner by a table of figures.*
– William Playfair

The contents of this book are meant to be modular – chapters can be used in any order, and individual Excel workbooks can be smoothly paired with any textbook. It could be argued, however, that this chapter on creating charts is a prerequisite to the study of economic models and data and, therefore, merits its leadoff status. A chart, also known as a graph, plot, or diagram, is so fundamental to the way economists visualize models and display data that it is often overlooked. Books present charts as if they were words, with no prior explanation, implicitly assuming that everyone knows how to read a chart. Using Excel to teach economics, with an emphasis on actively doing something rather than passively observing, forces explicit consideration of best practice methods for making a chart. Beginning with charting is an excellent way to introduce students to Excel and offers an opportunity to cover an ignored area of the undergraduate curriculum. The skills learned are sure to be used extensively in future courses and outside the classroom.

Students think that charting is trivial, but it is actually a complicated, serious matter, and there is, of course, a substantial literature on visualization and presentation of data. However, this is not a book about displaying data, so the optimal stopping point is reached quickly. A reasonable teaching goal is for a student to be able to produce a clear, basic graph in Excel. Be sure to emphasize that a guiding principle is to *minimize chartjunk*: irrelevant text, colors, or other visual elements that distract from and obscure the information being displayed. There is no doubt about it – a minimalist, simple approach is best.

Unfortunately, Excel is not helpful when it comes to creating a chart. It presents a bewildering array of chart types and options. Most students know that, in Excel, charts are created by selecting data, then clicking on a chart type button (or using the **Chart Wizard** button in older versions of Excel). Students need instruction, however, on exactly which chart type to use and how to best convey information. Creating a chart is a mix of art and science. Some things are just plain wrong, while others are simply ugly.

The work in this brief chapter proceeds in increasing order of difficulty. The first section walks through the process of making a chart in Excel and is easy enough to be suitable even for first-year students. To avoid tedious lessons on how to create a chart in Excel, simply send a student this link:

http://www.depauw.edu/learn/macroexcel/excelworkbooks/Charting/HowToChart .xls

The second section is more ambitious. It uses the *Econ Chart Enhancer* add-in to insert shaded bars in a scatterplot. This approach is often used to highlight recessions in a time series chart, and the add-in contains recession dates for the United States from the National Bureau of Economic Research. A second example is based on indicating high income inequality with shaded bars.

The *Econ Chart* add-in has a number of options that are not discussed in the screencasts for students. They are self-explanatory and briefly reviewed at the end of the chapter.

Sources and Further Reading

The epigraph is from William Playfair, *Playfair's Commercial and Political Atlas and Statistical Breviary*, edited and with an introduction by Harold Wainer and Ian Spence (1786; repr., Cambridge University Press, 2005), xii. Playfair invented graphical analysis, and his introductory comments reveal a deep appreciation of the power of visual representation:

> As the eye is the best judge of proportion, being able to estimate it with more quickness and accuracy than any other of our organs, it follows, that wherever *relative quantities* are in question, a gradual increase or decrease of any revenue, receipt, or expenditure of money, or other value, is to be stated, this mode of representing it is peculiarly applicable; it gives a simple, accurate, and permanent idea, by giving form and shape to a number of separate ideas, which are otherwise abstract and unconnected. In a numerical table there are as many distinct ideas given, and to be remembered, as there are sums, the order and progression, therefore of those sums are also to be recollected by another effort of memory, while this mode unites proportion, progression, and quantity, all under one simple impression of vision, and consequently one act of memory.

1.2

Simple Scatterplot and Double Y Charts:
HowToChart.xls

Chartjunk, says Tufte, generates "no information, no sense
of discovery, no wonder, no substance."
– James Surowiecki

Quick Summary

To access *HowToChart.xls*, visit: http://www.depauw.edu/learn/macroexcel/
excelworkbooks/Charting/HowToChart.xls

HowToChart.xls explains how to create various charts using Maddison
data on population, real GDP (in 1990 Gheary-Khamis (GK) dollars), and
real GDP per person for five Central American countries. This is a gentle
introduction to graphing in Excel, accessible to all students. You can assign
the workbook and safely count on the typical student being able to inde-
pendently complete the assigned tasks of creating several charts because the
student is asked simply to reproduce the screencasts.

Screencasts

- http://vimeo.com/econexcel/how-to-chart-in-excel: basic demo of how to create a
  chart in Excel
- http://vimeo.com/econexcel/chart-non-contiguous: charting when data are not
  next to each other
- http://vimeo.com/econexcel/using-series-formula: directly editing the SERIES
  formula in a chart
- http://vimeo.com/econexcel/double-y: make a chart with two y axes, one for GDP
  and the other for population
- http://vimeo.com/econexcel/real-gdp-per-person-instead-of-double-y: chart
  GDP/population for Costa Rica and Nicaragua
- http://vimeo.com/econexcel/five-countries-on-one-chart: chart of real GDP per
  person for five countries; using SERIES formula; amazing variation

Introduction

Students are not trained to produce charts. We simply expect them to pick it up as they go along. *HowToChart.xls* was designed to make sure students know how to create a properly labeled scatterplot in Excel. It can be used as a simple start to a course or as remedial instruction – send it to a student who cannot make a chart in Excel or who produces something so hideous that you have to turn away.

The highest priority message is to minimize chartjunk. Excel encourages all manner of distracting and confusing colors, markers, and shapes. Students love to express themselves with shading, shadowing, and word art. This combination can produce gaudy and bewildering output. Unless you are a professional, a clear, minimalist presentation is always best. A close second to minimizing chartjunk is to remember to clean up the chart. Excel's defaults are often undesirable, and axes labels are almost always needed.

If you do decide to use charting as a starting point for a course, note that the content is appropriate for economics. Instead of using hypothetical or random numbers, real-world data on population and output for Central American countries makes the work more interesting. This same strategy is used in the next section, which utilizes oil price and income inequality data.

Common Problems for Students

When charting in Excel, the two biggest problems to highlight to students are that (1) Excel will include a legend by default and will put down a generic "Series #" if no legend text is provided and (2) Excel can make poor initial choices for the graph, such as the maximum and minimum values of the axes.

Another source of confusion is the difference between a Line and a Scatter chart type. They seem like perfect substitutes, and students often select the Line chart type (perhaps because its icon looks like what they want to do), but these chart types are quite different, and because we are usually plotting numeric data, we will want to use the Scatter chart type. A Line chart is meant to be used when you have nonnumeric data on the x axis. It evenly distributes the categories (say, months of the year) on the x axis. If categories are not provided, Excel creates a default list. Much more common is the situation where we have numbers for all variables and we want to plot coordinate pairs. Unlike a Line chart, the scale of the x axis can be adjusted in the Scatter type. A good case can be made for simply ignoring this explanation and simply telling students, "Avoid the Line chart like the plague." It economizes on time, and you can be pretty sure that this advice will never cause a serious problem. Unfortunately, the FRED Excel add-in (covered in Chapter 4) uses the Line chart type.

One last area that can cause frustration arises when selecting the data that are to be plotted. A fundamental concept in Excel is that the CTRL key (or COMMAND key for Mac Excel) is used when selecting noncontiguous cells. I have actually seen students (and more than a few professors) literally move columns of data around in a spreadsheet to get columns next to each other because they did not know that holding down the CTRL key enables selection of cells anywhere on the spreadsheet.

Charting in Excel

Instead of just jumping in and drawing a graph, it is best to provide the student with a simple recipe for making a chart. There are three basic steps involved in making a chart:

1. Select the data.
2. Click a chart type button (almost always Scatter).
3. Clean up and improve the chart.

This recipe is applied repeatedly in the *HowToChart.xls* workbook. The *ToDo* sheet has the student create a series of charts based on Maddison data for Central American countries. The key idea to stress is to always examine the title, legend, and axis labels after Excel puts down the chart.

After creating a simple chart, the second task has the student chart data in noncontiguous (or nonadjacent) cells by holding down the CTRL key *after* selecting the first cell or group of cells. Holding down the CTRL key *before* you start selecting the data you want to graph is a common error and will seriously confuse Excel because you are including whatever cell you were on as part of the data to be charted. Remember, select the first cell or range of cells, *and then* hold down the CTRL key and select the next range.

A powerful way to make changes, introduced in task 2B (in the *ToDo* sheet) and repeated in task 4, is by directly editing the series. It helps to point out that, to Excel, data plotted in a chart are simply another function with output displayed in the chart. By selecting a plotted data series in a chart, the source data appear as a SERIES formula in the formula bar. Excel plots data as a SERIES formula with a structure like this:

= SERIES(legend text, x axis data, y axis data, series number)

You can copy a SERIES formula, then paste it and modify the arguments to add another series to an existing chart. Once you have a chart nicely formatted and set up as you like it, you can copy and paste that chart, then change the series simply by directly editing the SERIES function in the formula bar.

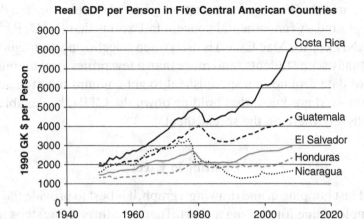

Figure 1.2.1. The answer to the final task.
Source: Produced with *HowtoChart.xls*.

The point is simple but powerful: Excel creates charts based on a SERIES formula that is similar to other functions in Excel. Once this is understood, charts can be copied and modified easily.

Double Y Chart

While scatter charts will probably occupy the vast majority of our charting life, the secondary *y* axis can be a useful tool. Task 3 shows how a second *y* axis can be easily added by right-clicking the series for which a secondary axis is to be used. The most important issue when using a secondary axis is to be sure that your audience can easily associate a series with its axis. If the context is clear, for example millions of dollars on one axis and interest rates on the other, no additional explanation may be needed. With GDP and population, it is not very clear which series belongs to which axis, so additional signage is needed to prevent confusion. Color is one option – make the series and corresponding axis the same color – but always remember that black-and-white printing will erase this signal. Arrows pointing from the plotted data to their axis is another option, although chartjunk starts to become a concern.

Task 3B tries to show that double Y charts can be complicated to read, and there may be easier ways to make the point. Instead of trying to show the relationship between population and real GDP on separate *y* axes, we can simply plot real GDP per person. This makes the point more much effectively than a double Y chart.

The final task in *HowtoChart.xls* has the student compare real GDP per person for all five countries. This gives the student a chance to practice some of the skills in the earlier tasks (especially working with the SERIES formula) and shows the amazing differences in economic performance over time – a crucial fact that every macroeconomics student should know. Figure 1.2.1 shows the finished product, with text boxes next to the plotted data for labels instead of a conventional Excel legend because this book is not printed in color. Students often overlook the fact that a chart in color can become impossible to read when printed in black and white – the strategy used in Figure 1.2.1 is an easy solution.

Conclusion

Charting is much underappreciated. The adage that a picture is worth a thousand words is really true when the chart is clear and well labeled. As charts get more complicated, their potential benefit rises, but so does the risk of confusion. Teach your students to keep charts simple and minimalist. For scatterplots, make sure that they avoid the Line chart type and smoothed Scatter options. Use legends only when more than one relationship is plotted, and never allow a Series # legend text to slip by.

The secret to good charting practice in Excel (and any other software) is to always remember the third step: *clean up and improve the chart.* Think of Excel's initial chart as a work in progress. One should always examine the initial chart with a critical eye. It is not necessary to add colors and other fancy aspects (and smoothing data is almost never a good idea), but always check to make sure you have a descriptive title and well-labeled axes and that the legend text is correct and needed. Best practice charting adopts a minimalist approach – always be on the lookout for ways to simplify the display and eliminate distraction.

Sources and Further Reading

The epigraph is from J. Surowiecki, "How Edward Tufte Led Bose Out of the Land of Chartjunk," *Metropolis* (1999), http://www.edwardtufte.com/tufte/metropolis_0199.

Jon Peltier's website on charting in Excel, http://peltiertech.com/Excel/Charts, is an excellent resource.

If you want more detail on the history of graphs and best practice charting, try these:

Klein, J. L. 2005. *Statistical Visions in Time: A History of Time Series Analysis 1662–1938.* Cambridge University Press.

Tufte, E. R. 1990. *Envisioning Information.* Graphics Press.

Tufte, E. R. 2001. *The Visual Display of Quantitative Information.* Graphics Press.

Tukey, J. W. 1977. *Exploratory Data Analysis*. Addison Wesley.

Wainer, H. 2000. *Visual Revelations: Graphical Tales of Fate and Deception from Napoleon Bonaparte to Ross Perot*. Psychology Press.

For a website dedicated to data display in economics, with an emphasis on income, visit http://visualizingeconomics.com.

1.3

The Shaded (Recession) Chart:
RecessionChart.xls and *EconChart.xla*

> (i). A *strongly good graph* shows us everything we need to
>   know just by looking at it.
> (ii). A *weakly good graph* shows us everything we need to
>   know just by looking at it, once we know how to look.
> – Howard Wainer

Quick Summary

To access *RecessionChart.xls*, visit:

http://www.depauw.edu/learn/macroexcel/excelworkbooks/Charting/
RecessionChart.xls

RecessionChart.xls uses real crude oil price data to demonstrate how to use
the *Econ Chart Enhancer* add-in to create a time series with shaded bars
based on U.S. recessions. It also uses World Top Incomes data to replicate a
chart on U.S. income inequality with shaded bars when the top 10% earn 45%
or more of total income. Proficiency with basic charting in Excel is required.

The *Econ Chart Enhancer* add-in, filename *EconChart.xla*, available
at http://www.depauw.edu/learn/macroexcel/exceladdins, enables enhance-
ments to an existing chart, such as natural log scale (not merely Excel's base
10 log scale) and easily adding shaded bars for recession (or other) time periods. Download the add-in from the website and use the Add-Ins Manager to
install it.

Screencasts

- http://vimeo.com/econexcel/howtoinstallexceladdin: shows how to install an add-
  in Excel via the Add-Ins Manager
- http://vimeo.com/econexcel/realcrudeoilpricechart: charts real crude oil price over
  time

- http://vimeo.com/econexcel/addrecessionbars: use the *Econ Chart* add-in to add recession bars to real crude oil price chart
- http://vimeo.com/econexcel/shadedbarswhenpricefalls: more practice with the *Econ Chart* add-in
- http://vimeo.com/econexcel/shadedbarsapplication: use the *Econ Chart* add-in to replicate a chart on income inequality

Introduction

Plotting a time series with shaded bars for recessionary periods has become a staple in financial literature. It is an effective way to show a second variable, such as the performance of the economy, while displaying more detail about a primary variable of interest. Unfortunately, it is not easy to create such a chart. Excel, however, can be tricked into doing it, and the complicated steps have been packaged into the *Econ Chart* add-in so the user can quickly add shaded areas to any chart.

Common Problems for Students

Installing the add-in requires use of the Add-Ins Manager. Students sometimes ignore all instructions and attempt simply to open the add-in file as if it were a conventional Excel workbook. This approach will not work. The distinction in the filename extension, .xls (or .xlsx, .xlsm) versus .xla, is apparently too weak a signal. If a student says the add-in does not work, the first question you should ask is, "How exactly did you install it?"

Of course, the add-in may be properly installed and there may be another issue causing a problem. The add-in does a variety of things, so there are many ways something can go wrong. It is usually helpful to have the student report exactly the steps the student took. A simple fix that seems to solve a lot of problems is to uninstall (uncheck the add-in and click **OK** in the Add-Ins Manager) and then reinstall (bring up the Add-Ins Manager dialog box and check the add-in).

Installing the *Econ Chart Enhancer* Excel Add-In

Excel add-ins are special files that provide additional functionality. After downloading the add-in file, the Add-Ins Manager is used to install it. The *EconChart.xla* file is available at http://www.depauw.edu/learn/macroexcel/exceladdins, and a screencast showing each step in the installation is available at http://vimeo.com/econexcel/howtoinstallexceladdin (this video link is also included in the *RecessionChart.xls* workbook).

Crude Oil Price Example

To pique interest and promote historical sensibility, a time series of crude oil price data serves as the canvas on which students can practice charting and enhancing the chart. The *RecessionChart.xls* workbook has instructions if you want to update the data or get more documentation and other variables. Hamilton (2011) uses these data and provides more detail on sources in his historical survey of the oil industry. Notice that dividing nominal ($ money of the day) by real ($ 2010) price yields the deflator, which could be used in a class presentation or as an assignment.

By working with real crude oil prices, students may be motivated to ask what drives prices and what will happen to the petroleum industry in the future. As Hamilton (2011, 18–19, footnote omitted) points out,

The last generation has experienced a profound transformation for billions of the world's citizens as countries made the transition from agricultural to modern industrial economies. This has made a tremendous difference not only in their standards of living, but also for the world oil market. A subset of the newly industrialized economies used only 17% of world's petroleum in 1998 but accounts for 69% of the increase in global oil consumption since then.

Oil price volatility in the last few years has been quite high, and students will be interested to see what has happened since 2010 (the last year in the workbook). This adds a sense of discovery and wonder to the assignments.

The first task is to update the data and create a simple chart of real oil prices over time. An easier version of this question would use the data in the workbook, but updating the data is not difficult. Once the chart is made, we are ready to enhance it with shaded bars to indicate recessionary periods, as shown in Figure 1.3.1. You would think this would be a difficult chart to make, but it is actually a double Y chart with the secondary axis suppressed. Other software (such as Stata) adopts this clever trick. The *Econ Chart Enhancer* add-in copies the chart to be enhanced (preserving the user's original chart) and applies the needed transformations. Notice that it actually creates a Line chart, so it will only work for time series (chronological, equally spaced) data.

The source for the shaded regions is a 0/1 dummy variable. The *Econ Chart Enhancer* has a user-defined function that enables the user to create the needed dummy variable for U.S. recessions (as determined by the NBER, of course). The screencast in the workbook shows how to use the RECESSION function for yearly data. For quarterly and monthly data, the function would be = RECESSION(cell address with date, "quarter") and = RECESSION(cell address with date, "month"), respectively. For daily data, no time period indicator is needed. For example, if you enter 10/1/2008 in cell A1

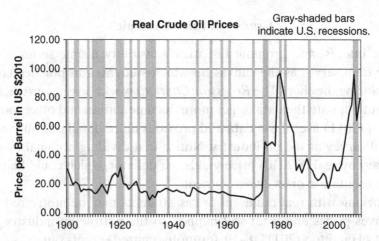

Figure 1.3.1. Oil price data with shaded recession bars (task 1B up to 2010).
Source: RecessionChart.xls.

and the formula = RECESSION(A1) in cell B1 (with the *Econ Chart* add-in installed), Excel displays "1" in cell B1 because the United States was in a recession on that date. This add-in will be updated regularly with new recession data for the United States, but the user can always manually enter 0/1 values for the latest values or other countries. .

Task 1C demonstrates that the shaded bars graph can be used for variables other than U.S. recessions. The user creates a 0/1 variable using an IF statement and then uses this variable to add shaded bars for years when the real price of crude oil was lower than the previous year.

Income Inequality Example

Given that income inequality dominates the news and will surely remain an important issue, the second example for charts with shaded bars is timely and interesting. Using the World Top Incomes database, the student downloads U.S. income data from 1913 to 2010 (or more recently, as the database is updated) and replicates a chart used in a *New York Times* article on inequality (Figure 1.3.2). Students should know that U.S. income inequality has markedly risen. Whether we want to do anything about that is a separate question, but as a matter of plain fact, the rise in inequality is not up for debate.

Although the data are not contained in the workbook, the screencast shows exactly how to download the needed series and compute the "Next 4%" and "Next 5%" variables. Once again, having to get the data adds an additional level of complexity, but the task is not difficult, and it is interesting to see how the latest values affect the story.

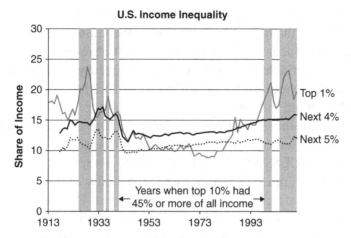

Figure 1.3.2. Replication of U.S. income inequality chart (task 2). *Source: RecessionChart.xls.*

This task presents a good opportunity to discuss how to document and manage data. After downloading the data, the workbook must be saved. File naming, which we often take for granted, deserves mentioning – saving the file as *Book3.xlsx* is not good practice. Data documentation, which is provided automatically in this case, should be augmented by the user with text boxes and comments about how the data were acquired and what was done. The screencast in the workbook does not mention either of these points.

Although economists (this author included) are probably not the best teachers of aesthetics and style, the use of shaded bars in Figure 1.3.2 to convey more information about the distribution of income and the strong visual message (with shaded bars on each end of the chart) are good lessons to point out. The simplicity of the variables used (as opposed to, say, the Gini coefficient) is another attractive feature of Figure 1.3.2.

The final task is open-ended, asking the student to add recession shading to a variable of his or her choosing. This provides the student an opportunity to do something creative and different from the usual, narrow question.

Conclusion

Making a chart with shaded bars for recessions (or another indicator) is easy with the *Econ Chart Enhancer* add-in. In addition to learning how to download and install an Excel add-in, your students will learn about oil prices and income inequality in the United States. They will be learning about charting, but not in a dry, humorless way with fake *x* and *y* data. The two examples can be used to stimulate discussion and present historical background, such as the rise of OPEC, the effects of fracking on oil prices, or how tax rates over time have affected the income distribution in the United States.

The World Top Incomes database is an excellent resource. It can be used to explore other variables and other countries. An easy assignment would be to have students create charts similar to Figure 1.3.2 for other countries and present and compare their work.

It is easy to use the *Econ Chart Enhancer* add-in to apply shaded areas to your data sets. Remember that the data must be sorted in chronological order, and the RECESSION function (included in the add-in) is a powerful way to quickly determine if a date or time period was in a U.S. recession. Another way to create a chart with U.S. recession bars is via the FRED add-in (discussed in detail in Chapter 4). After downloading data, click *Build Graph* and check *Include U.S. Recession Shading.* Click on the shaded areas in the resulting chart and examine the SERIES function to see that the *Econ Chart Enhancer* and FRED add-ins are using the same strategy to add recession bars to a chart.

Sources and Further Reading

The epigraph is from H. Wainer, "Graphical Visions from William Playfair to John Tukey," *Statistical Science* 5, no. 3 (1990): 341, http://www.jstor.org/stable/2245821.

The World Top Incomes database at http://www.wid.world/ is freely available.

For more on inequality, see T. Piketty, *Capital in the Twenty-First Century*, trans. A. Goldhammer (Belknap Press of Harvard University Press, 2014).

Hamilton, J. 2011. "Historical Oil Shocks." NBER Working Paper 16790. http://www.nber.org/papers/w16790.

1.4

Summary

New in Microsoft Excel 2010, a sparkline is a tiny chart
in a worksheet cell that provides a visual representation
of data.
– Office Documentation

This chapter manages to be both originally expansive and incredibly constrained. Economics professors do not bother to say anything about how to make a graph, so the slightest move in this direction is a radical departure, but there really is a vast world beyond the basic charts presented here. A course in macroeconomics is not the place to correct the graphing inadequacies of the typical undergraduate; however, it seems reasonable to insist on a properly labeled and titled time series chart. Naturally, because we are starting from zero, marginal returns are incredibly high, so anything we say about best practice graphing is bound to be valuable. In addition, the fundamental principles (especially minimizing chartjunk) do not change as we climb the ladder of data visualization techniques and methods.

For those interested in more advanced graphical techniques, here are three advanced tools for charting in Excel:

1. The *Econ Chart Enhancer* add-in, used to demonstrate recession shading, also has a variety of additional options, as shown in Figure 1.4.1. Any chart can be animated, and exponential growth curves can be fitted with growth rates displayed. These features, though reasonably self-evident, are demonstrated in the *MaddisonData.xls* workbook and Chapter 2. The add-in also has a zoom control (click the **Zoomer** button) that enables magnification of a portion of a chart. See the screencast at http://vimeo.com/econexcel/moneymsi for an illustration of how it works.
2. The *Histogram* Excel add-in, written by Frank Howland, is part of the suite of add-ins created for Barreto and Howland (2010). Excel's own histogram maker (included in the *Analysis ToolPak* add-in), putting the cart before the horse,

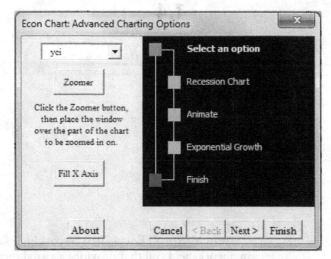

Figure 1.4.1. *Econ Chart* add-in main dialog box.
Source: EconChart.xla.

requires the user to set up bins before making the histogram. The *Histogram* Excel add-in, shown in Figure 1.4.2, eliminates all of these gymnastics. The user simply selects the data (one or two variables), and the add-in does the rest. It is freely available at http://www.wabash.edu/econometrics.

3. New in Excel 2013, the Office Store (in the Apps tab) offers a wide range of powerful mapping apps. The free Bing Maps app allows associating data with geographical locations and supports dynamic visualization (displaying data based on user input). Developers are producing new products at a rapid pace, so it pays to visit the Office Store to see the latest gadgets.

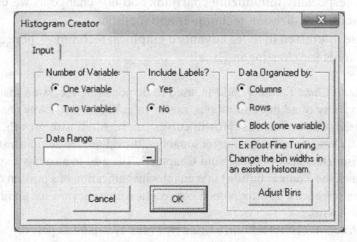

Figure 1.4.2. *Histogram* add-in main dialog box.
Source: Histogram.xla.

Visual representations of data have a long history. They allow for fast, intuitive understanding. It is obvious that we are moving to interactive visualization, with the display driven by user request. We are also seeing much more animation and movement in our graphs. A spreadsheet is perfectly positioned to take advantage of these trends. But no matter how technically sophisticated the software, with mind-blowing bells and whistles, the ability to communicate clearly will remain the ultimate goal. That seems a message worth sending – in every economics course we teach.

Sources and Further Reading

The epigraph is from http://support.office.com (goo.gl/jCU7Z8).

Barreto, H., and F. Howland. 2010. *Introductory Econometrics: Using Monte Carlo Simulation with Microsoft Excel*. Cambridge University Press. http://www.wabash .edu/econometrics.

2

Economic Growth Literacy

2.1

Introduction

> In fact, the main purpose of my work was not to provide a
> dataset for econometric work, but to encourage a younger
> generation to scrutinise the basic source material, try to
> improve its quality where it is weak, and to illuminate the
> underlying causes of growth and backwardness. This is
> why I took a lot of trouble to describe the sources and
> methods transparently.
> – Angus Maddison

Literacy can mean more than the ability to read. To be literate in a particular subject is to know and master a body of material. "The authoritative definition of economic literacy is knowledge of the theories that are held by professional economists" (Stigler, 1983, 65). Literacy in the subfield of economic growth is the fundamental pedagogical goal of the *MaddisonData.xls* workbook. The competency achieved by working through this material provides a launching pad for models and explanations of economic growth.

It takes repeated practice to attain literacy in every subject, but economic growth literacy is especially challenging because in addition to the historical record and facts, it requires numeracy – the ability to work with numbers and the mastery of fundamental mathematical tools. Thus, the workbook can be neatly divided into two parts. The first covers basic mathematical ideas such as the Rule of 70 and the interpretation of a log scale. The second focuses on historical trends and country comparisons. Both are embedded in the data to make the work interesting and thought provoking.

Maddison's Data

The data are provided by the monumental work of Angus Maddison, who spent his career painstakingly compiling measures of productivity and output across time and space. The *MaddisonData.xls* workbook contains

Maddison's original data, downloaded from http://www.ggdc.net/maddison, and adds buttons, scroll bars, and list boxes to make it easy to use and explore.

The *Doc* sheet contains complete documentation to download Maddison's original Excel workbook, *horizontal-file_02–2010.xls*, which contains the *Population*, *GDP*, and *PerCapita GDP* sheets. In addition to the obvious addition of buttons, scroll bars, and macros to the workbook, blank cells in these three data sheets were filled with #N/A.

Excel uses #N/A (not available) to signify that a value could not be found. An important and useful property of #N/A is that Excel will not plot such values. Maddison used blanks to denote missing values, but many Excel functions, including the SERIES function used in charts, treat blank cells as zero (Cryer 2001 severely criticizes Excel for how it handles missing data). We can take advantage of this behavior by replacing blanks with #N/A so that Excel will not plot a value of zero when a data point is missing.

While it is clear that several worksheets were added (i.e., *Intro*, *ToDo*, *Compare*, *Countries*, and *Doc*) to the original workbook, *MaddisonData.xls* also contains several hidden sheets. Right-click a sheet tab and select **Unhide** to reveal a hidden sheet. The *Norm* sheets contain data that are displayed when the ⎾ Normalize ⏋ button is used to compare countries from a common starting value of 100. The *Approx* sheet is made visible when the ⎾ Show %Change Approx Sheet ⏋ button (task 4 in the *ToDo* sheet) is clicked. The *CAGRAll* sheet has growth rates from 1950 to 2008 for all countries. The workbook also has two answer sheets, *ToDo7* and *ToDo8*, which are more concealed than simply hidden sheets. They can be displayed by running the *ToggleHideUnhide* macro, with keyboard shortcut CTRL-SHIFT-U. Worries about the unlikely possibility that students could access these answer sheets can be lessened by simply revealing and deleting these sheets before distribution.

Data Quality Issues

It is not necessary to alert beginning students to what can be sophisticated and difficult discussions regarding Maddison's estimates, but it is, of course, true that the data set has been the subject of scrutiny and debate. Broadberry (2013) argues that the latest scholarship points to much earlier roots for divergence and economic growth in Europe and Asia than Maddison's data would suggest. Galor (2011, 77) says,

The most comprehensive worldwide cross-country historical estimates of population and income per capita since 1 CE have been assembled by McEvedy and Jones (1978) and Maddison (2003), respectively. Indeed, despite inherent problems of measurement associated with historical data, these sources remain unparalleled in providing comparable estimates across countries in the past 2,000 years and have, therefore, been regarded as standard sources for such data in the long run growth literature. [Footnotes omitted.]

Acemoglu's (2009, 12) evaluation of Maddison's work points out weaknesses but ends on a positive note:

These data are less reliable than Summers-Heston's Penn World tables, since they do not come from standardized national accounts. Moreover, the sample is more limited and does not include observations for all countries going back to 1820. Finally, while these data include a correction for PPP, this is less complete than the price comparisons used to construct the price indices in the Penn World tables. Nevertheless, these are the best available estimates for differences in prosperity across a large number of nations beginning in the nineteenth century.

Summers-Heston Penn World Tables data on 189 countries for some or all of the years since 1950 are available here: http://cid.econ.ucdavis .edu/pwt.html. The OECD has data on purchasing power parity (PPP) and price comparisons for member countries at http://www.oecd.org/std/ purchasingpowerparitiespppsdata.htm.

In addition to the obvious decline in confidence the further back we go, estimates for the West are better than for other regions. Hansen (2002, 1257) correctly warns against the "natural tendency to regard all the data as of equal quality because it is published in the same place or as part of the same table." The twentieth-century numbers are reliable. "But his work for earlier periods remains problematic, although economic historians often find it too convenient to ignore as an input into their own research" (Hansen 2002, 1257).

Yes, the convenience of Maddison's data set is too strong to resist. It invites asking really big, long zoom questions, and for the purposes of stimulating interest in students, it has no rival. Maddison passed away in 2010, and the Maddison Project (see http://www.ggdc.net/maddison/maddison-project/ data.htm) hopes to continue updating and improving the data. The *MaddisonData.xls* workbook uses the last version Maddison published, with GDP up to 2008. The Maddison Project's GDP per person series goes up to 2010 and is included in the *PerCapita GDP* sheet starting in row 300. Compare, for example, China to see that substantial revisions have been made to Maddison's last published version. Working with these two data sets could provide the foundation for an independent study on measurement of real GDP.

Sources and Further Reading

The epigraph is from personal e-mail correspondence with Angus Maddison (1926–2010) on March 12, 2004. Visit http://www.ggdc.net/maddison to access his original home page and read tributes from students, colleagues, and friends.

Acemoglu, D. 2009. *Introduction to Modern Economic Growth*. Princeton University Press.

Broadberry, S. 2013. "Accounting for the Great Divergence." *VOX*. http://www .voxeu.org/article/accounting-great-divergence.

Cryer, J. 2001. "Problems with Using Microsoft Excel for Statistics." Paper presented at the 2001 Joint Statistical Meetings. Cryer correctly castigates Excel for its inconsistent and incorrect treatment of missing values. Although catchy and cute, "Friends Don't Let Friends Use Excel for Statistics" goes too far, in my opinion. It is better to know what the problems are and to avoid or fix them than to tell students not to use a product that is so dominant that they will almost certainly work with it every day.

Galor, O. 2011. *Unified Growth Theory*. Princeton University Press.

Hansen, J. R., II. 2002. "Review." *Journal of Economic Literature* 40, no. 4: 1256–57. http://www.jstor.org/stable/3217342.

Maddison, A. 2007. *The World Economy: A Millennial Perspective/Historical Statistics*. OECD. http://www.theworldeconomy.org.

Stigler, G. J. 1983. "The Case, If Any, for Economic Literacy." *Journal of Economic Education* 14, no. 3: 60–66. http://www.jstor.org/stable/1182859. Stigler concludes with a warning: "I do not despair of raising the economic literacy of the American public unless we fall prey to the superficial idea that all that is necessary is a course or two for every young American."

2.2

Setting the Scene

> Though the land were allotted to all men in equal
> amounts, only the strong would be able to keep their
> share. Though goods were allotted to all men in equal
> amounts, only the clever would be able to preserve their
> share. The clever can make profits ten times their outlay,
> but the stupid cannot even retain their capital. If the
> sovereign cannot regulate (the making of profits), the
> people's living standards will vary over a range in which
> one has a hundred times as much as the other.
> – Guanzi

Economic growth literacy begins with the amazing fact that, when considered on a human history time scale, economic growth is brand new. Many of us take this knowledge for granted, but most students have never explicitly been made aware of this fact or considered its implications.

We manage to explain that economic growth is measured by the percentage change in real GDP per person but often fail to highlight how different the last few hundred years have been from everything that went on before. The rise of the market system and its ability to produce sustained increases in real GDP per person over long periods of time is a critical difference in kind and degree that must be brought front and center.

Depending on how you unveil it, you might get a gasp from Figure 2.2.1. This hockey stick graph is a great way to open any presentation on economic growth. It captures attention and provides a memorable image that reinforces the stunning discontinuity in output per person. It allows the very first message, something different happened suddenly and output per person exploded, to be the most important thing you communicate. Everything else is commentary, mopping up operations revolving around this most critical fact about the historical record.

Students are completely blind to the fact that, on a time scale of millennia, the market system has been in use only for several hundred years. Note that

World Average

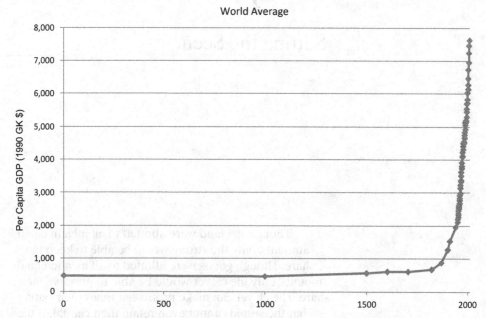

Figure 2.2.1. Real GDP per person over two thousand years.
Source: MaddisonData.xls.

neither money nor trade (including bazaars and other marketplaces) is sufficient for a market system. Cuba has not one but two simultaneously circulat-
ing currencies and many stores with people paying with cash, yet everyone
would agree that it does not have a market system.

While macroeconomics is neither economic history nor history of economic thought, students have to be taught that the market system slowly
evolved in Europe after the discovery of the New World. By the time Adam
Smith wrote *Wealth of Nations* in 1776, he could see that England and a hand-
ful of other European countries were much richer than they had been before
and they were rapidly separating themselves from the rest of the world. Smith
correctly attributed what he saw as a stunning economic performance to the
market system, a decentralized form of organization that relied on prices to
signal resource allocation, profits to spur innovation, and self-interest to elicit
effort. The emergence of protected property rights and growing freedom
of individual choice (especially for labor markets) were critical institutional
developments. Of course, Smith was writing at the dawn of the British Industrial Revolution, when output per person especially accelerated as mecha-
nization and factories sent productivity soaring relative to past experience
(but disappointing by today's standards).

It is the fact that per capita GDP started growing a few hundred years
ago after millennia of stagnation that needs to be emphasized in a macroeconomics course (and in introductory economics). This can be demonstrated

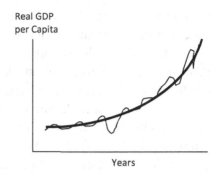

Figure 2.2.2. Stylized graph of a market economy.

with strong visuals (such as Figure 2.2.1) and supporting computations using Maddison's data set. In conjunction with the data analysis, basic mathematical tools for the study of growth can be utilized and explained.

In addition to the novelty of economic growth, a clear separation must be made between short run, cyclical versus long run, path analyses. This critical difference can be easily captured by a stylized graph, as shown in Figure 2.2.2.

Draw the thin, squiggly line first, highlighting the ups and downs of the business cycle (with a serious crash representing a Great Depression) and then "fit" a thick line through the data to represent the long-run path of the economy.

Point out that the thin, squiggly line is the actual, observed performance of the economy, which bounces above and below its trend. Macroeconomics separates analysis of fluctuations and stabilization, with its primary focus on the booms and busts of a market economy, from the long run, which is especially concerned with explaining and influencing the trajectory of the path over long periods of time.

The Most Important Open Problem in Economics

There is pedagogical danger in presenting Figure 2.2.1 because students immediately ask what caused output per person to rocket, and frankly, we do not know what produced modern economic growth beyond the grossest generalizations. We know it was the evolution of the market system, but it gets cloudy beyond that. Yes, rule of law in protecting private property is vital, but exactly, specifically which laws, and why, we cannot say.

I do not recommend denying that economics is ignorant since the truth is that we just do not know. Instead, turn it around and make it a challenge. Why some countries grow and become rich while others are poor is the most important open problem in economics. Lucas (1988, 5) drills it when he says, "Is there some action a government of India could take that would lead the Indian economy to grow like Indonesia's or Egypt's? If so, what exactly? If not, what is it about the 'nature of India' that makes it so? The consequences for human welfare involved in questions like these are simply staggering: once one starts to think about them, it is hard to think about anything else."

If you go down the rabbit hole of defining the market system, there are many ways to provoke your students. One especially intriguing idea is that it is financial innovation, specifically a stock market, which is the core of the market system. While Adam Smith was severely critical of joint stock companies, highlighting what we would today call the principal-agent problem (Smith [1776] 1904, V.1.107), Schumpeter ([1911] 1934) went so far as to claim that credit is the essence of capitalism. The entrepreneur is, of course, the innovative force that drives economic growth, but access to finance is a necessary condition for the market system to deliver sustained material progress. Most people view the stock market as a rigged casino, but this totally misses its crucial role as financial intermediary in channeling savings to investment. The ability to amass and allocate large pools of money capital is a tremendous boon to entrepreneurs, feeding the perennial gale of creative destruction.

Since money has been around for a long time and people have exchanged things for millennia, it is obvious that mere trade is not a perfect marker of a market system. Heilbroner (1953, 312–13) defines it as everyone having license and desire to maximize: "I ask the reader only to remember that never before, in any society, had the pursuit of wealth been legitimated, much less celebrated, for everyone. Kings, of course; adventurers, perhaps; the lower classes – never." The timing is certainly right, but then again, could it be that the creation of the Dutch East India Company in 1602, which issued shares of stock that were traded on the Amsterdam Stock Exchange (the first stock market), was also a critical mutation that drove the evolution of what we now see as modern capitalism?

For a quick, two-minute video that describes the creation of the joint-stock company and the stock market, visit http://vimeo.com/econexcel/firststock. It is guaranteed to brighten up an introductory lecture on stocks. Ferguson (2008) has more detail and explanation, if needed.

A Brief History of the Concept of Economic Growth

Another angle on growth that students will find interesting is its treatment by scholars over time. Arndt (1978, 5) pointed out that "the idea of material progress as a possible or desirable human condition does not, in western thought, go back much beyond the beginning of the eighteenth century." It is only when real GDP per capita started to rise that a higher standard of living became desirable and needed an explanation, along with a corresponding mechanism by which policy could stimulate increasing output.

The classical economists, from Smith to Mill and Marx, focused on growth and saw capitalism as an innovative, dynamic system. The Marginal

Revolution in the 1870s turned attention to static optimization and markets as a resource allocation mechanism. From then until the Great Depression, economic growth essentially disappeared from mainstream economics.

The worldwide economic collapse in the 1930s caused a revolution in the discipline of economics, and economic growth suddenly returned to the main stage, but the birth of national income statistics also played a critical role. For the first time, we would have data with which to measure growth. Arndt (1978, 21, footnote omitted) credits Colin Clark (*National Income and Outlay* published in 1936) as "probably the first to think in terms of an 'annual rate of growth of real income per head of the population' and to try to estimate this magnitude statistically." After World War II, growth theory and empirical analysis really took off. The Solow Model gave us an iterative, dynamic process by which to understand long-run growth, and it led to a wide variety of extensions and econometric analyses, continuing to the present day.

Why Do We Want Economic Growth?

To recap, by the eighteenth century, the market system had evolved to a stage where sustained growth was observable and people began to think of material progress as desirable. A seventy-year interlude was followed by the rise of growth theory after World War II. In both the initial and modern phases of focus on growth, there have been constant and sharp criticisms of the desirability of rising real GDP per person as a goal and the costs associated with growth.

Inequality in distribution of output has always been a problem, as has the pain caused by rapidly collapsing industries. The evils of urbanization, environmental damage, and worries about the future of humans and the earth itself are persistent criticisms of economic development. At the deepest level, we can question the fundamental purpose of growth, highlighting its unsatisfying materialism and ultimate meaninglessness.

Lewis (1955, 420–21) still has the best case for growth:

The advantage of economic growth is not that wealth increases happiness, but that it increases the range of human choice. ...We certainly cannot say that an increase in wealth makes people happier. We cannot say, either, that an increase in wealth makes people less happy, and even if we could say this, it would not be a decisive argument against economic growth, since happiness is not the only good thing in life. ...We do not know what the purpose of life is, but if it were happiness, then evolution could have stopped a long time ago, since there is no reason to believe that men are happier than pigs, or than fishes. What distinguishes men from pigs is that men have greater control over their environment; not that they are more happy. And on this test, economic growth is greatly to be desired. The case for economic growth is that it gives man greater control over his environment, and thereby increases his freedom.

Robbins (1934, 142–43) reminds us that some of the issues are beyond the bounds of economics and that it is easy for the rich to trade growth for other desirable ends, forgetting the many who are still poor:

But do we want economic progress in this sense? This is clearly a question of ultimate valuation upon which neither economics nor any other science is capable of giving a decision. All that science can do is to present the alternatives. The ultimate decision is one of will, not of knowledge. But, if a digression into this sphere be permitted, it does seem pertinent to observe that the majority of the human race are still very poor and that if, in the interests of a supposed stability, a halt is to be called in the process of raising real incomes, it is an issue which should be squarely presented to those who are most affected by it. It is all very well for the dilettante economists of wealthy universities, their tables groaning beneath a sufficiency of the good things of this world, their garages furnished with private means of transport, to say, "Food is cheap enough. Charabancs [a large bus, typically used for sightseeing] are vulgar. The railways are admirable. We have enough of plenty. Let us safeguard security." It is for the millions to whom a slice of bacon more or less, or a bus ride to the sea, still matter, to make the decision.

Real GDP per person is far from a perfect measure of economic performance, and there are critics who reject increasing it as a policy objective. It remains, however, a dominant statistic, and the most common way to assess the functioning of an economy. High annual rates of growth have produced spectacular success in Vietnam, driving the poverty headcount from 58% in 1993 to 16% in 2006 (Baulch 2011, 246). To these tens of millions of people lifted out of poverty, any debate over economic growth is nonsensical – it is a godsend.

Sources and Further Reading

The epigraph is from Lewis A. Maverick's *Economic Dialogues in Ancient China: Selections from The Kuan-Tzu* (Southern Illinois University Press, 1954), 117, originally written about 300 BCE. Guanzi (the pinyin translation of Kuan-Tzu) is a text often attributed to Guan Zhong, but most scholars today believe it is a compilation of material from a variety of authors.

Arndt, H. 1978. *The Rise and Fall of Economic Growth: A Study in Contemporary Thought*. Longman Cheshire.

Baulch, B. 2011. *Why Poverty Persists: Poverty Dynamics in Asia and Africa*. Edward Elgar.

Ferguson, N. 2008. *The Ascent of Money: A Financial History of the World*. Penguin. A full set of freely available videos is available at http://www.pbs.org/wnet/ascentofmoney.

Heilbroner, R. 1953. *The Worldly Philosophers: The Lives, Times, and Ideas of the Great Economic Thinkers* Simon and Schuster. 7th ed. published 1999.

Lewis, W. 1955. *The Theory of Economic Growth*. Gorge Allen and Unwin.

Lucas, R. 1988. "On the Mechanics of Economic Development." *Journal of Monetary Economics* 22:3–42.

Robbins, L. 1934. *The Great Depression*. Books for Libraries Press. http://mises.org/books/depression-robbins.pdf.

Schumpeter, J. (1911) 1934. *The Theory of Economic Development: An Inquiry into Profits, Capital, Credit, Interest, and the Business Cycle*, trans. Redvers Opie. Harvard University Press.

Smith, A. (1776) 1904. *An Inquiry into the Nature and Causes of the Wealth of Nations*. Methuen. Full text at http://www.econlib.org/library/Smith/smWN.html.

2.3

Attaining Economic Growth Literacy:
MaddisonData.xls

> Another [major innovation] had its origin in the need for
> rapid computation with theoretical consequences which
> no one could have foreseen when Napier, a Scotsman, and
> Bürgi, a Swiss, respectively and independently published
> in 1614 and 1620 the first account of what the former
> called *logarithms*.
> – Lancelot Hogben

Quick Summary

To access *MaddisonData.xls*, visit

http://www.depauw.edu/learn/macroexcel/excelworkbooks/MaddisonData.xls

MaddisonData.xls includes data on population, real GDP (1990 international
Gheary-Khamis dollars), and real GDP per capita on many countries stretching back
to the year 1 CE. The *Compare* sheet in the workbook offers a simple yet powerful
interface to compare countries, which provides a strong visual presentation to stimulate meaningful questions.

Screencasts

- http://vimeo.com/econexcel/maddisondataintro: how to use the workbook, highlighting growth as the most important open problem in economics
- http://vimeo.com/econexcel/measuringgrowth: computing growth via annual percentage change and compound annual growth rate for U.S. real GDP per person;
  demos **Data Vertical** button and Equation Editor
- http://vimeo.com/econexcel/logscale: showing how a log scale reveals if something
  is growing at a constant rate
- http://vimeo.com/econexcel/ruleof70: explaining the Rule of 70 and applying it to
  U.S. real GDP per person
- http://vimeo.com/econexcel/percentagechangeapprox: simple numerical example
  and concept applied to Australian real GDP, population, and real GDP per person

- http://vimeo.com/econexcel/seeminglysmalldiffgrowthrates: seemingly small differences in growth rates create huge gaps over time
- http://vimeo.com/econexcel/tremendousvariability: large variation in real GDP per person; sorting data
- http://vimeo.com/econexcel/growthnotgiven: sorting and Excel's RANK function used to show that early fast growers are not guaranteed to continue growing fast
- http://vimeo.com/econexcel/worldshares: charting shares of world output for the United Kingdom, the United States, and China

Introduction

Economic growth literacy requires numeracy. There are fundamental concepts such as percentage changes and knowledge of what is fast and slow growth that can only be developed through example and practice. Working with Maddison's data should relieve some of the tedium.

The screencasts have a sequential order. The first is a general overview, the next four cover mathematical tools, and the rest review the historical record. Skipping one or two from the last group is reasonable, but the others are core material that should be a part of even the most spartan coverage of economic growth.

Common Problems for Students

Curves can be hard to read. A curve growing at a constant rate is flat on the left and steep on the right, and many students incorrectly interpret this as growing slowly at first, then rapidly. Pointing this out early on can help them understand the mechanics of growth. Ironically, once a student learns about growth, he or she often makes the opposite mistake, seeing every curve as growing at a constant rate.

The typical undergraduate student will have had little practice with growth rates, log scales, and simple rules of thumb, such as the Rule of 70 and the percentage change approximation. Appreciating the power of compounding – that seemingly small differences in growth rates produce huge disparities over time – and developing the ability to approximate the time needed to double are fundamental concepts that cannot be ignored.

Using *MaddisonData.xls* in the Classroom

The ability to quickly compare countries was the original objective in creating this workbook, and the simplest, easiest pedagogical use of this workbook is to display the *Compare* sheet while lecturing. Use the buttons and other tools along the sides and bottom to modify the chart as needed. If you create something you want to keep, simply copy the sheet and rename it. This can be done as many times as needed since Excel can store literally thousands of sheets in a workbook.

The *Compare* sheet can be used to study an individual country and explore its economic history or to race countries against each other. In either case, switching from population, real GDP, and real GDP per person is easily controlled by clicking one of these choices in the **Set Variable** box below the list of countries.

While there are many interesting countries to choose, including recent high performers, such as Ireland (before the real estate collapse) and Botswana, and less fortunate countries (e.g., Venezuela), perhaps the highest value in terms of individual countries to study would come from examining the United States and China.

A chart of real GDP per person in the United States during the twentieth century is certainly familiar to every economist and that alone is a good argument for presenting it to our students. Such a chart highlights the Great Depression and makes it easy to discuss the business cycle versus the long-run path (especially if you add a fitted line). Specific time periods can be highlighted and growth rates quickly displayed. After they get comfortable with the American historical record, switching to a log scale gives students practice reading such charts.

Schumpeter ([1942] 1976, 66), joining a long line of those impressed by the power of capitalism, was awed by America's growth from 1870 to before the Great Depression: "One way of expressing our result is that, if capitalism repeated its past performance for another half century starting with 1928, this would do away with anything that according to present standards could be called poverty, even in the lowest strata of the population, pathological cases alone excepted." In class or as an assignment, the *Compare* sheet can be used to quickly show that the compound annual growth rate for real GDP per person actually increased from 1.72% between 1870 and 1928 to 2.08% between 1928 and 1978. Apparently, our standards for poverty have changed.

Going forward, Gordon (2010, 24) forecasts a pessimistic 1.5% annual growth rate in real GDP per person in the United States, which he notes "falls far short of the historical achievement of 2.17 percent between 1929 and 2007 and represents the slowest growth of the measured American standard of living recorded during the past two centuries." Gordon (2012) follows up with a "provocative," "unorthodox," and "audacious" idea – economic growth was a one-time-only event produced by one-time-only innovations. But Brynjolfsson and McAfee (2014) completely reject Gordon's pessimism, arguing that we are at the dawn of new era of phenomenal growth. The fact that forecasts are so wildly different is not surprising given that we do not understand the details of why and how growth actually works. The charts and analyses Gordon offers apply the tools used in the *MaddisonData.xls* workbook and could be used in a debate format or assigned as a response paper.

The last task in the *ToDo* sheet shows how China's share of world output was high, fell, and now has risen again, but the *Population* and *PerCapita GDP* sheets also reveal interesting aspects of Chinese history and can be used in a variety of ways in the classroom. Chart real GDP per person in the *Compare* sheet and zoom in to pinpoint China's takeoff from 1978's opening and reform. Coase and Wang (2012), Hu (2011), and Lin (2012) are excellent sources for learning about the Chinese economy and the transition from a planned economy to a market system.

The Chinese economy has been growing extremely rapidly for more than three decades (although precisely estimating output is complicated by quality of data issues, see Rawski (2001)). This sustained speed and longevity are unmatched for such a large country. Lin (2012, 264) is absolutely right when he says that "600 million people were lifted out of extreme poverty," so we can conclude that "Chinese reform and achievements can be called a miracle in economic history." Coase and Wang (2012, 202) are no less effusive:

What had happened in China since the death of Mao is certainly breathtaking. China today would hardly be recognized by Mao if he walked out of his mausoleum. He would be astounded to find out that private entrepreneurship and free markets could actually realize his broken dream, one shared by the Chinese people for more than a century, of remaking China a rich and powerful nation.

Showing students a chart of the recent explosive growth of China's economy will beg the critical question, What will happen going forward? The answers are varied (indicative of how little we know), and Fogel (2010, 70) offers a provocative prediction:

In 2040, the Chinese economy will reach $123 trillion, or nearly three times the economic output of the entire globe in 2000. China's per capita income will hit $85,000, more than double the forecast for the European Union, and also much higher than that of India and Japan. In other words, the average Chinese megacity dweller will be living twice as well as the average Frenchman when China goes from a poor country in 2000 to a superrich country in 2040. Although it will not have overtaken the United States in per capita wealth, according to my forecasts, China's share of global GDP – 40 percent – will dwarf that of the United States (14 percent) and the European Union (5 percent) 30 years from now. This is what economic hegemony will look like.

Few students can resist the exciting and inspiring ideas that the data and charts make clear. Displaying *MaddisonData.xls* is an easy, powerful way to enhance a lecture and capture your students' attention.

In addition to individualized analysis, cross-country comparisons are an especially potent way to teach about modern economic growth and the amazing variability in outcomes. The introductory screencast (http://vimeo .com/econexcel/maddisondataintro) has a series of examples starting at the 6:45 mark that invite questions such as, Why is Slovenia so much richer than the other former Yugoslav countries? and Why did Botswana take off while its neighbors languish? Here are other cross-country questions one can explore:

> When did the United States pass England?
> How did Germany and Japan do before and after World War II?
> Are the Asian Tigers all doing about the same, or is there variability there also?

Thought-provoking questions about growth and stagnation are everywhere and can be used at the introductory level or in more advanced courses. If you trust your students, let them loose and ask them to explore their own countries and frame their own questions. You may be pleasantly surprised – using these data, my students have made such interesting comparisons as the United States and the United Arab Emirates, Asian subcontinent countries, China and Cambodia, Spain and Argentina, and Ghana and Nigeria. International students especially are often unaware of their native country's history and are eager to see how neighboring countries fare against their homeland. Student presentations, of course, would be another option.

Finally, the *MaddisonData.xls* workbook can be used to replicate Galor's (2011) comparison of the timing of the takeoff across regions and add country takeoffs to the presentation. Chapter 2, "From Stagnation to Growth," in Galor (2011) provides an excellent overview of world economic history and is a great help for content and display ideas for an introductory lecture on growth. Galor's home page at http://www.econ.brown.edu/fac/Oded_Galor has several resources, including lecture slides.

Tasks in the *ToDo* Sheet

Tasks are organized into two groups: numeracy and economic literacy. The former includes mathematical concepts needed to work with the data, while the latter begins the process of understanding the patterns in the data, emphasizing the tremendous variability in outcomes in the last few centuries.

Percentage change and compound annual growth rate (CAGR – the measure displayed by the Show Ann % button on the *Compare* sheet) are explained in the first task. CAGR is more challenging, of course, than the percentage change, but the step-by-step explanation (including using the Equation Editor) and application of the CAGR formula to a concrete example will enable many students to master the concept.

The second task points out that a log scale can be used to determine if something is growing at a constant rate – if it is linear on a log scale, the rate of growth is constant. This task uses Office's **Drawing Tools** to create an arc (showing students how to draw in Word and Excel) and shows that although it is a curve, it is not growing at a constant rate. Senegal's population was chosen as the assignment because it did grow at a roughly constant (and extremely fast) rate of 2.8% per year from 1950 to 2008. Another nice application of the log scale is for Japan's real GDP per person from 1950 to 2008 – it is easy to see the break in growth rate in 1973, and close inspection reveals an even more serious slowdown dating from 1991.

The Rule of 70 is reviewed in the third task by constructing a simple example and testing how well the approximation works, then applying it to real GDP per person in the United States. In addition, the screencast points out that the approximation is better the smaller the constant rate of growth and describes 2% per year growth in real GDP per person as excellent performance for a developed country.

The Rule of 70 is simply stated and not derived. It follows directly from the equation of exponential growth $X_t = (1 + r)^t X_0$, where r is the growth rate and t is the time period. Since we want to know how long X takes to double, we write $2X_0 = (1 + r)^t X_0$ and, therefore, $2 = (1 + r)^t$. Taking the natural log (ln) of both sides yields $\ln 2 = t \ln(1 + r)$. Two approximations are now utilized: (1) $\ln 2 \approx 0.70$ and (2) $\ln(1 + r) \approx r$, for small r. Substitute in the two approximations and multiply both sides by 100 to get $70 = tr$, where r is now expressed in percent, and solve for the time it takes to double as $t = 70/r$. This is the Rule of 70. This derivation could be assigned as homework, although it is easy to find on the Internet, along with other versions, for example, the Rule of 72 (which has more factors than 70).

The final numeracy task is devoted to the percentage change approximation. By changing a cell value, it is easy to show how the approximation works and that the smaller the percentage change, the better the approximation. The Data Vertical button is used to get data on Australia and show that the annual percentage change in real GDP per person is roughly equal to the percentage change in real GDP minus the percentage change in population.

Having acquired a few basic math tools, the focus turns to literacy about economic growth. The fundamental fact – that modern economic growth began a few centuries ago, after millennia of stagnation – has already been stated in the introductory screencast. The four tasks on economic literacy are grouped around variability in outcomes. As presented in the introductory screencast, our lack of understanding of the mechanisms driving growth should not be downplayed; instead, we should encourage work on the biggest open problem in economics – why are some countries rich and others poor?

We begin by developing sensitivity to the importance of seemingly small differences in growth rates. The entire real GDP per person sheet is copied and sorted by year 1900 real GDP per person. Countries with missing data are removed and the CAGR from 1900 to 2008 is computed. This enables comparison of countries that had similar real GDP person in 1900 and is a powerful way to display the divergence that occurs from seemingly small differences in growth rates. The task asks the student to compare Norway and Greece, and the standard answer would attribute Norway's success vis-à-vis Greece to the growth rate, but a more nuanced answer would point out that Norway's real GDP per person was over 40% higher in 1900 – something hard to tell from the chart in the *Compare* sheet.

To emphasize the importance of seemingly small differences in growth rates in a classroom setting, show that a geometric progression is multiplicative and, therefore, more powerful than an arithmetic (additive) sequence. By starting from a blank worksheet and doing the work right before their eyes, you can develop deep appreciation for the outcomes produced by geometric sequences. Begin by asking your students to choose one of two options at the end of one year: add $1 million per day to $1 or have it grow at 10% per day. This is a hard question since it seems obvious that the huge head start of $1 million additively gives an overwhelming initial advantage to the arithmetic sequence, but then again, students know you are trying to explain the power of compounding. If you ask them to just rely on intuition, most students would choose the $1 million per day. The question can be answered easily with a spreadsheet. To see the simple instructions, unhide the *Sequences* sheet (right-click any sheet tab and select *Unhide*).

The live demonstration in class, which takes a short time to set up, can really impress students. They are shocked at the power of the geometric sequence, and a chart comparing the two is also quite compelling. You can further prod them by stating the following amazing claim: no matter what constant amount and growth rate you choose, the multiplicative series will eventually catch up and pass the arithmetic series. Once the sheet is set up, it is easy to show that seemingly slight differences in the constant rate of growth have a huge effect over time. Change the rate of growth to, say, 11% and note the impact this has at the end of the year.

Task 6 uses two user-defined functions, MAXOFCOUNTRIES(cell range, TRUE if suppress Kuwait, Qatar, and UAE) and MINOFCOUNTRIES(cell range), to add these two variables to the data and include them in the list box in the *Compare* sheet. This enables bounding the chart in the *Compare* sheet with the max and min values for real GDP per person. Now, when a country is added to the chart, it is displayed in context with the highest, average, and lowest real GDP per person. The tremendous variability in outcomes after the advent of modern economic growth is now striking.

The next task continues the focus on variability by comparing growth performances at the beginning and end of the twentieth century. CAGR is used to compute growth from 1900 to 1930 and from 1970 to 2000. After sorting the data based on growth from the first period and removing missing values, Excel's RANK function is used to show that early fast growers do not repeat their success. Venezuela drops from first to last. China does the reverse. Run the *ToggleHideUnhide* macro, with keyboard shortcut CTRL-SHIFT-U, to display the *ToDo7* sheet to see the answer to the task.

The final task compares the very-long-run performance of the United Kingdom, the United States, and China in terms of their contributions to world GDP. The Data Vertical button is used to obtain data on the three countries and world GDP. Shares are computed (and relative as opposed to absolute references are explained). In the screencast, a chart of the shares displays the results, and the discussion covers the role the United Kingdom, the United States, and China play in the global economy over time. Running the *ToggleHideUnhide* macro displays the *ToDo8* sheet, which has the answer to the task. The screencast ends with a brief discussion of valuing output with PPP versus market exchange rates. For living standards, PPP seems the obvious choice; but for measuring contribution to world output, the appropriate measuring stick is much less clear. The Organisation for Economic Co-operation and Development website on PPP is an excellent resource for further study on price differentials across countries: http://www.oecd.org/std/purchasingpowerparitiespppsdata.htm.

Sources and Further Reading

The epigraph is from Lancelot Hogben's *Mathematics for the Million*, 4th ed. (1937; repr., W. W. Norton, 1968), 402.

Brynjolfsson, E., and A. McAfee. 2014. *The Second Machine Age: Work, Progress, and Prosperity in a Time of Brilliant Technologies*. W. W. Norton & Company.

Coase, R., and N. Wang. 2012. *How China Became Capitalist*. Palgrave Macmillan.

Fogel, R. 2010. "123,000,000,000,000." *Foreign Policy* (Jan/Feb) 177: 70–75. http://www.foreignpolicy.com/articles/2010/01/04/123000000000000.

Gordon, R. 2010. "Revisiting U. S. Productivity Growth over the Past Century with a View of the Future." Working Paper 15834, NBER. http://www.nber.org/papers/w15834.

Gordon, R. 2012. "Is US Economic Growth Over? Faltering Innovation Confronts the Six Headwinds." Policy Insight 63, CEPR. http://cepr.org/active/publications/policy_insights/viewpi.php?pino=63.

Hu, A. 2011. *China in 2020: A New Type of Superpower*. Brookings Institution Press.

Lin, J. 2012. *Demystifying the Chinese Economy*. Cambridge University Press.

Rawski, T. 2001. "What's Happening to China's GDP Statistics?" *China Economic Review* 12, no. 4: 347–54. http://www.pitt.edu/~tgrawski/papers2001/gdp912f.pdf.

Schumpeter, J. (1942) 1976. *Capitalism, Socialism and Democracy*. George Allen and Unwin.

2.4
Summary

The central issue is the effects of the number of people upon the standard of living, with special attention to raw materials and the environment. On balance the long-run effects are positive. The mechanism works as follows: Population growth and increase of income expand demand, forcing up prices of natural resources. The increased prices trigger the search for new supplies. Eventually new sources and substitutes are found. These new discoveries leave humanity better off than if the shortages had not occurred.
– Julian L. Simon

Acemoglu (2013, 170) makes a strong case for changing content: "The thesis of this article is that the amount of time spent teaching growth and development at the undergraduate level should be increased, both because it is of interest to students and because there is lots of exciting research going on in the area that is teachable to undergraduates, unlike research in many other areas of economics." *MaddisonData.xls* provides a convenient, low-cost way to enact this change.

Basic economic growth literacy about the world and individual countries can be quickly and interestingly conveyed with *MaddisonData.xls*. This workbook can be used to enhance a lecture or tasks can be assigned as homework or in a lab setting (see Barreto and Widdows 2010 for an economic growth lab). Your students will master fundamental mathematical tools and gain an appreciation of how economists routinely use growth rates and log scales. Perhaps more importantly, you can forcefully, visually show how modern economic growth exploded on the scene just a few centuries ago as the market system evolved.

Lost in this exciting story is the distribution of output. By dividing real GDP by population, we implicitly convey the impression that individuals receive average shares of output, and this is patently false. Perhaps the best example of this is Equatorial Guinea: it boasts the highest growth in per capita real GDP from 1950 to 2008 in the data set (chart it in class from the *Compare* sheet to raise a few eyebrows), but the oil revenue that drives this growth is concentrated in a few hands. We need theory about and data on the distribution of output. This needs to be said, but it remains true that fast growth will solve many distribution issues.

If you insist that distribution must be included in any discussion of growth (a perfectly valid position), Piketty (2014) is an excellent, accessible, data-driven resource. Online technical appendixes include a variety of Excel workbooks with data and detailed source notes. The World Top Incomes database at http://www.wid.world/ makes it easy to download data in Excel and compare countries over time. Unhide the *Future* sheet in *TechProgress.xls* to see a brief explanation of how low *g* affects inequality.

The *MaddisonData.xls* file has perhaps the greatest potential of all of the Excel workbooks described in this book – in the hands of a good teacher, it can be used to arouse tremendous passion and elicit sincere effort from students. The screencasts merely scratch the surface of what can be accomplished with *MaddisonData.xls*.

Sources and Further Reading

The epigraph is from Julian L. Simon's *Ultimate Resource 2*, rev. ed. (Princeton University Press, 1996), 579, available at http://www.juliansimon.com/writings/ Ultimate_Resource. Simon was well known for his contrarian views and challenging his opponents to wagers. His most famous bet was with ecologist Paul Ehrlich, a modern Malthusian who was convinced human population growth would soon destroy the Earth. In 1980, Ehrlich chose five commodity metals and bet Simon that their prices would rise over the decade, signaling increasingly scarcity as human consumption outran production. Simon won the wager, but this settled nothing – the difference in worldview between economists and ecologists remains as wide as ever.

Acemoglu, D. 2013. "Economic Growth and Development in the Undergraduate Curriculum." *Journal of Economic Education* 44, no. 2: 169–77. http://www .tandfonline.com/doi/abs/10.1080/00220485.2013.770344.

Barreto, H., and K. Widdows. 2012. "Introductory Economics Labs." *Journal of Economic Education* 43, no. 1: 109. http://www.tandfonline.com/doi/abs/10.1080/ 00220485.2012.636717. Lab 10 is on economic growth using Maddison data.

Piketty, T. 2014. *Capital in the Twenty-First Century*, trans. A. Goldhammer. Belknap Press of Harvard University Press.

3

The Solow Model

3.1

Introduction

> Before presenting the Solow model, it is worth stepping
> back to consider exactly what a model is and what it is for.
> In modern economics, a model is a mathematical
> representation of some aspect of the economy. It is easiest
> to think of models as toy economies populated by
> robots. ...The best models are often very simple but
> convey enormous insight into how the world works.
> – Charles Jones

Consider this discussion, versions of which have been played out countless times in faculty offices around the world:

PROFESSOR: Welcome. How can I help you?

STUDENT: I am having trouble with the Solow Model. It is confusing.

PROFESSOR: Yes, this is a difficult model. What exactly is the problem?

STUDENT: I can see how increasing the rate of population growth (n) or the depreciation rate (δ) will hurt the economy –

PROFESSOR: The nifty canonical graph, also known as the Solow diagram [which the professor quickly sketches as in Figure 3.1.1], makes that obvious, don't you think? The line rotates up and steady-state capital per worker in efficiency units falls, so steady-state output and consumption per worker in efficiency units will also fall. Ta-da!

STUDENT: I see that for n and δ, but g is where I get really baffled. Why would technological progress *hurt* the economy? Shouldn't an increase in g help, with more consumption as we produce more output with the same resources?

PROFESSOR: You are forgetting that the x axis on the canonical graph is capital per worker in *efficiency units*. That's not the *actual* economy –

STUDENT: I know that. You emphasized this point a lot in class. But here's my question then: *Where is the actual economy*? How can I see what is happening there? Does the canonical graph have some secret trap door that reveals the impact of g on the economy itself, not in efficiency units but in actual output per worker?

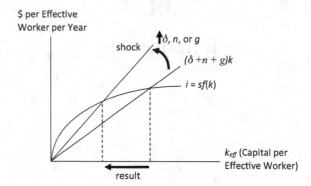

Figure 3.1.1. Comparative statics with the Solow diagram.

PROFESSOR: Um, no, there are no secret trap doors. The canonical graph just provides
an ingenious way to find the steady-state in a model with constant technological
progress. That is all it does. To figure out what is happening in the actual economy,
you have to transform each variable back into its own, nonefficiency units, ideally
in a time path chart. So, even with n and δ, strictly speaking, we should not be
making claims about what is happening to the actual economy based on what we
see in the canonical graph. We have to do the transformation to see the effect.

STUDENT: OK, but how do I do that? Our book doesn't do that. I tried to look in
other books and none of them do it either.

PROFESSOR: Yes, I agree that professors tend to hand wave at this point and just make
claims that everyone memorizes for the exam, but let's give it a shot. Imagine you
had a spreadsheet or some software that tracked the path of the actual economy
after an increase in g. What do you think the path would look like?

STUDENT: Are you serious? I have absolutely no idea. It is ridiculous to expect someone to perform such amazing feats of transformation. You are asking me to imagine time paths for several variables ($k, y, c,$ and i) with a shock to the rate of technological progress, ceteris paribus, including a transition period as the economy
converges to its new steady-state? That is impossible. I doubt that even Gauss or
Ramanujan could do this. [Clearly this is no typical undergrad.] Wouldn't it be
better if we had the computer simply display the results? You should develop an
Excel file that does this.

PROFESSOR: Yes, yes, you are quite right – that would be helpful indeed …

Although no student ever challenged me on the standard exposition in quite
this way, the hypothetical conversation above contains an essential truth – it
was frustration with the fundamental confusion caused by Figure 3.1.1 that
led me to implement the Solow Model in Excel. It seemed to me almost unfair
to require such fantastic feats of imagination by the student. If you really want
the typical undergraduate to understand the properties of the Solow Model,
you have to eliminate abstraction and make the presentation concrete. This
can be done with simulation. The student will see, on his or her screen,
the time path of key variables in the economy and no superhuman feats of

imagination are required. Cranking out the evolution of capital, output, consumption, and investment year after year is extremely tedious by hand and ridiculously easy with a computer. A button click is all that is needed. Comparative statics becomes a matter of merely changing a variable and seeing what happens to the simulated economy.

At the undergraduate, textbook level, there is little debate about the model itself, and this makes using the Excel implementation of the Solow Model seamless with almost any macro text. Mankiw (2013) put growth theory into the forefront of the intermediate macroeconomics course in 1991 with the debut of his macro text that featured the Solow Model at the beginning of the book. This was a radical departure from the mainstream, which focused heavily on the short run and stabilization policy – growth, if covered at all, was an afterthought tacked on at the end.

Today, many intermediate macro texts, following Mankiw's lead, cover the long run first, and then turn to fluctuations. After reviewing the historical record, with emphasis on growth and variability in output per person, the conventional textbook exposition features the Solow Model as the starting point of theoretical work. The production function, laws of motion, and the steady-state solution are presented with equations and graphs.

My Excel implementation of Solow's growth process closely mirrors the established content, but the delivery is markedly different. As has become standard practice, the Solow Model is presented here by building gradually from the mechanics of capital accumulation to a model with population growth and technological progress. Putting all of this material into a single Excel file would overwhelm the student. Thus the exposition of the Solow Model is rolled out as a series of four Excel workbooks:

1. *KAcc.xls* is the basic model of capital accumulation, with emphasis on how capital makes output, which is then split into consumption and investment for next year.
2. *GoldenRule.xls* shows how steady-state consumption per worker depends on the saving rate. This leads to the idea that there is an optimal s that maximizes c. Simulation shows how increasing the saving rate to its Golden Rule level requires a transition period of temporarily lower consumption per worker.
3. *Population.xls* contains both data and theory. It uses Excel to directly download data from the U.S. Census Bureau to create population pyramids. It also augments the *KAcc.xls* model with positive population growth.
4. *TechProgress.xls* extends the model again, this time incorporating positive technological change. This is the Solow Model with exogenous growth.

These workbooks should be done in sequence and require at least one class period per workbook. The last two are difficult, and there is enough material to devote more time to these workbooks. *Population.xls* can be split into demographics and theory, while *TechProgress.xls* could be spread over

Class	Excel	Description	Highlights
1	*KAcc.xls*	Introduction	Steady-state solution via time path, then Solow diagram
2	*KAcc.xls*	Comparative Statics	s and δ effect on k^*, y^*, c^*
3	*GoldenRule.xls*	Choose s to max c^*	Time path makes transition transparent
4	*Population.xls*	Demography	Data on population pyramids and growth rate
5	*Population.xls*	Adds n	Using Excel's Scenario Manager for comp statics
6	*TechProgress.xls*	Adds g	Time paths for imaginary and actual economies
7	*TechProgress.xls*	Comparative Statics	Capital destruction and real-world data

Figure 3.1.2. Example curriculum for Solow Model coverage in a macro course

several class days. The mathematics of the model is presented in separate sheets in the workbooks to enable a completely graphical and simulation-based exposition. Discrete time is used throughout. For details on the differences and implications of continuous versus discrete time, along with discussion of numerical solution issues, see Novales et al. (2009).

Many screencasts are included in these four Excel workbooks. A complete listing, organized in sequence within each workbook, is available at http://www.depauw.edu/learn/macroexcel/screencasts. If time is especially tight, the Golden Rule workbook can be skipped without loss of continuity.

Figure 3.1.2 shows an example timeline for using these files, assuming one-hour-long classes in a macro topics course. Visit http://www.depauw.edu/learn/macroexcel/coursematerials to download a zip archive with handouts for each class. These handouts contain additional material and can be easily modified. They were used in a flipped classroom environment, so you can see how in-class time was devoted to problem solving and discussion.

Why the Solow Diagram and Simulation?

Simulation is a powerful way to teach the Solow Model, but it is not meant to eliminate conventional emphasis on the Solow diagram. Instead, the canonical graph that is often merely memorized can finally be shown to be what it is – a remarkably clever device to solve the model. Likewise, analytical solutions can be confirmed via simulation.

It is best to think of simulation as a complement rather than a substitute for traditional expositions relying on graphs and equations. The goal, to teach the model, is the same as it has always been. We want our students to understand and find the steady-state solution and perform comparative statics analyses. Simulation is an additional means to these ends, offering students another bite at the apple.

The Solow diagram itself is a classic graph that plays an important role in the explanation of the model. By showing the change in k as the gap between the investment curve and ray out of the origin, the iterative logic is laid bare. Another strong point is that it reveals the equilibrium solution in an instant. Given our discipline's emphasis on visual representation, the Solow diagram deserves its place in the pantheon of canonical graphs, such as supply and demand, marginal revenue and marginal cost, and indifference curves and budget constraint. Simulation will help students master the Solow diagram and truly understand the family of models known as the Solow Model, which is the workhorse apparatus of growth theory.

In the handouts mentioned earlier (Class 3 in Figure 3.1.2), there is a nice example of the power of simulation. In class, a student asked if the transition effects of the Golden Rule could be mitigated by gradual increases in the saving rate. Subsequent discussion ended with three proposals for taking the economy in *GoldenRule.xls* from the initial $s = 30\%$ to its Golden Rule value of 50%:

1. Cold turkey: the usual immediate, one-time shock in s from 30% to 50%
2. Gradual: s rises by 1% point every other year until it reaches 50%
3. Really slow: s rises every ten years by 1% point until it reaches 50%

The Solow diagram is not much help in evaluating these alternatives, and I was completely unaware of the subtleties involved, but my students used simulation to produce time path graphs and tables that enabled rich discussion (see the Golden Rule section for results). The striking part was that we were all over the map on what would happen, but once we started simulating, we had data to look at and we could see the positives and negatives of each proposal. It was a wonderful class because we figured out a complicated question, and it seemed that everyone in the room was invested and able to understand what we were doing.

Sources and Further Reading

The epigraph is from C. Jones, *Introduction to Economic Growth*, 2nd ed. (W. W. Norton, 2001), 21. Jones's presentation of the Solow Model is clear and accessible to undergraduate students, which is also true of Mankiw and Weil:

Mankiw, N. 2013. *Macroeconomics*. 9th ed. Worth. The parameter values for the initial problem in the workbooks (always available by clicking the [Original Example] button) are from Mankiw.

Weil, D. 2013. *Economic Growth*. 3rd ed. Prentice Hall.

For more advanced, graduate-level expositions of the Solow Model, see

Acemoglu, D. 2008. *Introduction to Economic Growth*. Princeton University Press.

Romer, D. 2012. *Advanced Macroeconomics*. 4th ed. McGraw-Hill.

For a presentation with special emphasis on numerical methods, see

Novales, A., E. Fernández, and J. Ruíz. 2009. *Economic Growth: Theory and Numerical Solution Methods*. Springer.

3.2

Capital Accumulation: *KAcc.xls*

> Moreover, the production function has been a powerful
> instrument of miseducation. The student of economic
> theory is taught to write $O = f(L, C)$ where L is a quantity
> of labour, C a quantity of capital and O a rate of output of
> commodities. He is instructed to assume all workers alike,
> and to measure L in man-hours of labour; he is told
> something about the index-number problem involved in
> choosing a unit of output; and then he is hurried on to the
> next question, in the hope that he will forget to ask in
> what units C is measured. Before ever he does ask, he has
> become a professor, and so sloppy habits of thought are
> handed on from one generation to the next.
> – Joan Robinson

Quick Summary

To access *KAcc.xls*, visit

http://www.depauw.edu/learn/macroexcel/excelworkbooks/SolowModel/KAcc.xls

KAcc.xls includes several sheets that carefully explain capital accumulation
in a basic version of the Solow Model (no population growth or technological
progress) and an *EqPath* sheet that enables quick simulation of an economy,
along with a series of charts to display results.

Screencasts

- http://vimeo.com/econexcel/kacc: introduces the Solow Model and shows how to
  use the *EqPath* sheet to run a simulation and find the steady-state solution
- http://vimeo.com/econexcel/kacccs: copies the *EqPath* sheet and does comparative
  statics analysis via direct comparison of two economies

Introduction

To teach the Solow Model effectively, the material must be chopped into bite-sized pieces. *KAcc.xls* introduces the model, focusing on the core, iterative mechanics at the heart of the model. It also shows how capital accumulates when starting below the steady-state, and then settles into a repetitive pattern that is the hallmark of the steady-state. This simple model can generate only catch-up growth (with no growth in the steady-state), so it is clearly a stepping-stone that must be extended to exhibit persistent, long-run growth.

Common Problems for Students

Not only are almost all students unfamiliar with dynamic models, most find the notation of the Solow Model to be a significant barrier. Solow (1956) cleverly transformed a two-variable, L and K, system into a single variable, $k = K/L$, model, but undergraduate students tend to overlook the levels versus per worker distinction in the variables. It is important to continually stress and write out the variables, for example, "output per worker," instead of merely using y.

An associated difficulty is that Solow diagram, the canonical and fundamental solution graph (top right in Figure 3.2.1), relies on capital per worker driving investment and depreciation. While the latter is straightforward, investment depends on the saving rate and productivity, which can be confusing. Not only do students have to understand how the steady-state will be reached, but they must be able to shift curves as various shocks are applied. Simulation offers an excellent way to teach the steady-state and comparative statics because the student works first with graphs of key variables over time. A graph of y, c, and i over time is natural to read and clearly shows the steady-state value of a variable as a flat line (top left in Figure 3.2.1). The information on the chart over time can be compared to the more difficult to read Solow diagram. This approach, examining variables over time before turning to the canonical graph, can also be used to explain how comparative statics shocks affect the steady-state solution. With the information from the simulated paths easily available, the student learns how to read and use the canonical graph.

The two bottom graphs in Figure 3.2.1 depict other ways to explain and understand the steady-state. The bottom left chart shows that savings equals investment in the steady-state and the change in k is zero. The bottom right chart is quite advanced. It is a type of phase diagram, useful for exploring the properties of equilibration. Several reviewers encouraged addition of a graph showing the growth rate of y over time. This graph lives below the bottom left

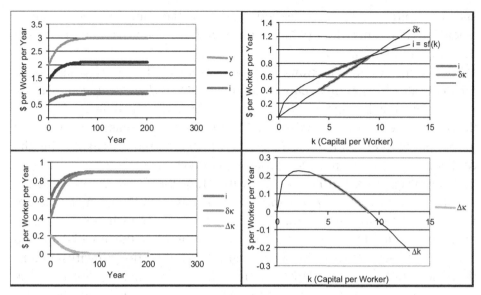

Figure 3.2.1. Solow Model graphs.
Source: Top charts in *EqPath* sheet in *KAcc.xls* after simulating 200 years.

chart in each of the Solow workbooks. It is not included or mentioned in any of the screencasts.

You may strongly prefer a different arrangement of graphs, perhaps promoting the growth rate of *y* chart, for example, above the frozen pane in the worksheet in favor of the graph above it or the phase diagram. That is no problem. You may rearrange the charts in any fashion (but do not delete any of them because some buttons will no longer function properly). All formatting, including color and line styles, can be modified to your liking. Move the legends to the bottom; add titles; or resize the charts. This is one of the advantages of delivering material this way – do not hesitate to adjust and reorganize the charts to suit your preferences. Just click on the chart to select it and drag it where desired. If you think four charts are too many, drag two far right, where they will not be seen.

Unlike supply and demand, which is familiar to students, the Solow diagram is a new graph that requires slow presentation when first encountered. Repetition will develop proficiency in working with Solow's original display of the model's solution, but exceedingly careful exposition at first contact with the Solow diagram is certainly a best practice.

For example, it makes sense to describe the units of the axes in the Solow diagram. This is not, however, as straightforward as it seems. Solow (1956, 66) sidestepped Robinson (1953–54) and the capital controversies by positing that "there is only one commodity, output as a whole, whose rate of production is designated $Y(t)$." Everything – output, consumption, investment, and the capital stock – is measured in units of the composite good. Solow labeled his diagrams with r (which is our k, K/L) on the x axis and $\dot{r}$ (the time derivative of r) on the y axis.

Something got lost in translation to textbooks. The y axis had to be renamed, and most authors chose axis labels such as *depreciation* and *investment* to describe the functions being graphed, instead of dealing head-on with the issue of the units of the axis itself. *Change in k* makes sense as a label until output per worker is added to the graph, which then requires explaining the confusing fact that capital and output are equivalent.

The top right chart in Figure 3.2.1 (like all of the Solow diagrams in the Excel workbooks) uses *$ per worker per year* based on the normalization of $1/unit for the composite good. This causes no confusion when y is added to the graph and has the virtue of a smooth transition when the model is applied to real-world data. Also, Robinson's epigraph to this section notwithstanding, the typical student is helped by thinking of the x axis as an input level (a stock of capital per worker at a point in time) that drives the functions displayed in the graph, producing flow measures of value on the y axis.

The Structure of the Model

Conventional notation and definitions of variables are used (enabling pairing with most textbooks) and explicitly presented in the Excel workbook. The exposition is heavily focused on the mechanics of the model, so supplementary text or lecture notes may be needed to fill in background information. You can modify the notation and add your own material in text boxes as needed.

The law of motion of the capital stock at time t, K_t (with an initial amount of capital, K_0, given) is

$$K_{t+1} = K_t + I_t - \delta K_t,$$

where δ is the depreciation rate of capital each period and I_t is investment per period, given by

$$I_t = sY_t,$$

where s is the saving rate and Y_t is total output per period, given by a constant returns to scale (CRS), Cobb–Douglas production function:

$$Y_t = AK_t^\alpha L_t^{1-\alpha}.$$

Dividing by L_t (which is constant for every time period) and backward substituting yields the capital stock law of motion in the per worker version of the model:

$$k_{t+1} = k_t + sAk_t^\alpha - \delta k_t,$$

with the steady-state equation (or equilibrium condition) being

$$\Delta k = sAk_t^{\alpha} - \delta k_t = 0.$$

Solving for k yields the steady-state solution (see a detailed derivation in the *Algebra* sheet):

$$k^* = \left(\frac{sA}{\delta}\right)^{1/1-\alpha}.$$

Steady-state solutions for other variables can be found by simply evaluating variables at k^*.

Presenting the Model to Students

The *Intro*, *ConsInvFn*, and *Steady-state* sheets lay out the model. The *Intro* sheet introduces the cyclical logic of the model with a simple flow chart. The text emphasizes the split in output into consumption and saving (which automatically equals investment). It concludes by encouraging the student to click on the [Setting Things Up] button, which offers a simple example where the student must read pop up boxes and click to see what happens the next time period. The student will walk through a few cycles of k producing y, which is then split into c and i, with i added to k for next period's production.

The *ConsInvFn* sheet begins by repeating the flow chart and then transforming it into per worker variables. The text explains how a CRS, Cobb–Douglas production function allows for such a transformation and walks through the algebra. The consumption and investment functions are then presented.

The *Steady-state* sheet introduces the idea of depreciation and stresses the equilibrium condition, including a description of what happens when k is above and below its steady-state value. This sheet also includes explanatory notes and definitions, such as the meaning of investment and the distinction between stocks and flows. The sheet ends with a discussion of growth as percentage change versus a high level of output per person.

Although the philosophy of these materials is based on strong visuals, these three sheets are heavily laden with text because students need repetition from alternative presentations of the cyclical logic of a growth model. The [Setting Things Up] button offers yet another way to see how the model works and can be used in a class lecture to walk through a few time periods. You can use these sheets as supplements to your favorite textbook exposition or notes, offering them as optional supporting resources. If you think they are a distraction, hide or delete them.

Finding the Initial Solution

The simple algebra of the model would seem to suggest writing equations as a convenient way to present the model to students, but a series of mathematical statements is not the best way to teach this model. It requires too much attention to notation and is too abstract for beginners. Drawing graphs of production, investment, and depreciation functions then combining them in the Solow diagram is the usual approach, but it still suffers from the fact that the student must conceptualize the motion generated as the model cranks out results period after period.

Simulation offers an introduction to the model that is exceptionally user-friendly because of its concrete, visual exposition. This enables deep understanding of the mechanics of the model as well as its canonical solution graph. Thus, after reviewing the variables and functions (either in class or from the workbook), the best place to start is by using the *EqPath* sheet to show that the economy is attracted to its steady-state solution.

The screencast at http://vimeo.com/econexcel/kacc shows how the *EqPath* sheet could be used in a lecture. Begin by clicking on each cell in the first year (used instead of the more abstract "time period"), from B14 to H14, revealing each formula and explaining what is being computed. Then walk through a few years of the model, one year at a time, by clicking on the `1 Year` button. The charts come to life, plotting the data from the simulation. Having shown how each cell is computed and how each row adds another year, click the `? Years` button and answer 200 when asked how many years to run the simulation. Focus on the *y*, *c*, and *i* over time (top left) chart first because it is the easiest to understand, but be aware that the top right chart, where the canonical graph is displayed, is the eventual goal. The bottom right graph is included as another way to convey the solution as the point where $\Delta k = 0$. It is only briefly mentioned in the screencast.

Notice that data from the simulation are being plotted on the charts on the right, which is useful for explaining how these charts work. Emphasize that the steady-state is reached when the variables repeat themselves, and stress how this occurs at the intersection of the two functions on the canonical graph. Picking a year and showing how the values for that year are plotted on each chart is a good way to connect the charts and firmly establish the relationship between the time paths on the left and standard graphs on the right. The charts are easily modified (changing colors or using dashed lines, for example) or can be rearranged to your liking. This flexibility is one of the great advantages of using Excel to deliver content.

The screencast points out that simulation will not always produce an exact answer. A good rule of thumb is to drive Δk to a small number, at least to 10^{-5} or 10^{-6}. Excel uses scientific notation, 1.234E-05, for example, when the number becomes too small to display in the cell. The simulated cells in the *EqPath* sheet are not formatted with $, even though these are their units, to allow the user to see the economy converging to the steady-state. Usually, displaying so many decimals places is distracting, but the use of simulation as a solution strategy means that rounding is not a good option.

Students sometimes run the economy for enough years that Excel shows zero for Δk (in column H) and believe this is an exact answer. In fact, this may or may not produce the exact solution. It does for the parameters of the original problem (after 650 years or so), but, depending on parameter values, Excel may simply not have enough precision to continue approaching the true, exact steady-state and may compute zero instead of the correct, small number. In the screencast, a randomly generated parameter set produced endless repetition at 10^{-16}, and Excel could get no closer. Further muddying the waters is the fact that a machine with infinite memory and precision would never reach the steady-state via simulation. When Excel does show zero, it may be an accidental result caused by limited precision – the change in k is so small that Excel treats this extremely small number as zero.

These computational issues are shrugged off in the screencast because they are not important for the task at hand. Simulation is being used here to demonstrate the mechanics of the model, and it will produce a sufficiently good approximation to the exact answer for any parameter set. Worrying about answers that may be off by miniscule amounts is akin to spending hours teaching the difference between the t and normal distributions with sample sizes in the thousands. As the screencast says, the point is that simulation displays convergence, and this is what helps students understand the model. For more details on numerical simulation and methods, see Novales et al. (2009).

For students who want more detail on the limitations of simulation, an easy way to explain the inability of iteration to produce an exactly correct answer in every case is to connect the model in Excel to penalties in an American football game. If the defense is offside with the ball on their own 1 yard line, applying the half the distance to the goal penalty puts the ball on the half-yard line. If the defense is offside again, the referee will place the ball on the quarter-yard line. This process would continue forever and the ball would never reach the goal line. (A clever ploy, albeit rarely used, would be for a defensive player to charge across the line, pointing at the offensive player and claiming that he moved first – after all, the half-distance-to-the-goal cost pales in comparison to the potential gain of moving the ball back to the six yard line.) Just like the ball will never reach the goal by repeated halving, Excel will never reach the steady-state by iteration. If this fails to convince your student, assign a paper on Zeno's Paradox.

One extension not covered in the screencast is adding a time series for k to the top left chart, as shown in Figure 3.2.2. The sheet will still work, but

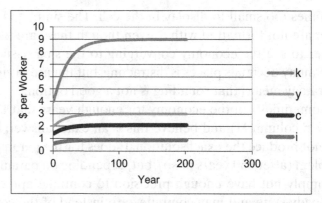

Figure 3.2.2. Adding *k* over time to the *yci* chart.
Source: Top-left corner chart in *EqPath* sheet in *KAcc.xls*.

this added series will not automatically update (like *y*, *c*, and *i*), thus, it is best to add this series after driving the economy to its steady-state solution. In a lecture, you could ask students what *k* will look like after it is added, and then add it. The other series will be scrunched together, and pointing out that the *y* axis scale has changed may be helpful. Adding *k* could also be assigned as homework.

Another feature not discussed in the screencasts is the Play ▶ button. It changes the SERIES formula to plot one data point at a time, producing the animation effect. The speed depends on your computer and the number of years simulated. Press the ESC key to interrupt the macro and click **End** if it is taking too long. In a lecture, talking and describing what is going on during the animation can be quite effective.

The Rand button is an excellent way to generate new problems. It enables quick display of new parameter sets so students do not fall into the habit of simply memorizing the solution values for the original problem. In a lecture, this button provides endless examples and, as homework (e.g., task 4), you are assured that students are not simply copying a friend's work.

The algebraic solution to the model is presented in the *Algebra* sheet. It is reasonably straightforward, and when exogenous variable values in cells B31:B34 are changed, the steady-state solution in cells B38 and B42:B44 update. This material can be skipped with no loss in continuity.

Comparative Statics

After the mechanics of the model are mastered and the steady-state solution is found, comparative statics, as usual, is next on the agenda. The screencast at http://vimeo.com/econexcel/kacccs offers a gentle introduction to comparative statics analysis in this model. As with the initial solution, instead of mathematics or the Solow diagram, data from the simulation forms the foundation of the comparison before and after the exogenous shock. The screencast explores how changes in *s* affect the steady-state solution, and task 6 examines the effect of δ, so shocks to *A* or α could be used in class or as an alternative homework assignment.

The strategy adopted in the screencast is based on copying the *EqPath* sheet, changing *s* to 40% in the newly created sheet, and directly comparing the initial and new sheets. While obviously a cumbersome approach, this does have the benefit of clarity and showing how the entire path is affected by a shock to one variable. The screencast points out that although raising the saving rate will produce a higher steady-state *c*, consumption per worker is initially lower because a greater share of output is saved. Introducing students to transitional dynamics early on will pay dividends when explaining the Golden Rule because students will have seen that consumption per worker depends on the saving rate.

Using the Solow diagram to shift either the investment or depreciated capital per worker functions is the common approach to comparative statics in this model. This method is used in the next workbook, *GoldenRule.xls*, where the *CS* sheet enables changing a parameter and clearly shows the shift in the chart. A good case can be made, however, that faster is not better in this case because the student needs time to absorb how the model works. The lack of familiarity with the model and difficulty in reading the canonical graph requires a slower initial pace, and the student needs to see the steady-state solution a few times. Shifting curves immediately after introducing the Solow diagram is likely to result in confusion and memorization.

Tasks

The tasks in the *ToDo* sheet closely follow the screencasts. The first three tasks require the student to explore the role of *Initial k*. The discovery that the steady-state solution is unaffected by the starting value of capital per worker, reinforces the meaning of the steady-state. The second task demonstrates another concept not covered in the screencasts, the trajectory of the economy when *k* starts above the steady-state. By simply changing cell B10 so that it is greater than the steady-state value of *k*, the student can see how the equilibration process works in this case. The graphs over time show the variables gradually decreasing to their steady-state values and the canonical graph shows how the intersection is reached by moving *k* from right to left. The growth rate of *y* chart, not included in the screencast, shows zero percentage change in *y* in the steady-state, no matter if we start above or below k^*.

Task 4 uses the | Rand | button to have the student produce a unique economy. Showing that each parameter configuration produces its own steady-state is not a trivial point to make.

Tasks 5 and 6 focus on comparative statics. The former asks the student to repeat the analysis in the screencast (except *s* falls to 20%), and the latter explores the effect of a change in δ. As mentioned earlier, examining the effect of *A* and α is also a possible homework or exam question. Additional ways to do comparative statics are discussed in the next workbook, *GoldenRule.xls*.

The last two tasks use the algebraic solution to replicate the answers obtained via simulation, showing that the two approaches do, in fact, yield the same results. These tasks require a bit more mathematical background for successful completion.

Conclusion

The Solow Model cannot be taught in a single class. Appropriate pace is needed. The *KAcc.xls* workbook does not try to do too much. It focuses on two things: the cyclical logic of the model and the steady-state solution. It is important to make clear and repeat the distinction between levels of capital (*K*), output (*Y*), consumption (*C*), and investment (*I*) versus their per worker versions, *k*, *y*, *c*, and *i*. Take the time to walk through the cells in the *EqPath* sheet and repeat several times how *k* makes *y* (via the production function), which is then split into *c* and *i* depending on *s*. Investment per worker adds to *k* while depreciated *k* is subtracted, leaving a Δk that may be positive or negative (depending on the value of *k* vis-à-vis steady-state *k*). This process and the explanation of each step should be repeated several times.

The *Final* sheet in *KAcc.xls* has a summary of important points, including the fact that this simple model will not produce sustained economic growth. You can use the growth rate of *y* chart (which is not shown in the screencast) to make this point clear. In the steady-state, *k* unchanging means that *y* is constant and the percentage change of *y* is zero. This model can display growth as the economy approaches its steady-state path, but once there, growth stops. Therefore, capital accumulation alone does not produce persistent increases in output.

Like all of the Solow Model workbooks, *KAcc.xls* is flexible and adjustable. You can rearrange the charts to your liking and modify markers and colors as needed. You can create alternative parameter sets quickly and easily. Remember that you can copy the *EqPath* sheet repeatedly to save your favorite scenarios and examples.

Of course, the comparative statics properties of the model are significant and worth extended discussion, but they are gently introduced at this point, including the idea of transitional dynamics. The next workbook in the Solow Model series, *GoldenRule.xls*, explores the effect of changing *s* in detail.

Sources and Further Reading

The epigraph is from J. Robinson, "The Production Function and the Theory of Capital," *Review of Economic Studies* 21, no. 2 (1953–54): 81, http://www.jstor.org/stable/2296002. This is a key paper in the decades-long Cambridge capital controversies and Robinson pulls no punches, with her first sentence claiming that the dominance of the neoclassical production function "has had an enervating effect upon the development of the subject."

The *Final* sheet in *KAcc.xls* provides the citation for the original version of the model: R. Solow, "A Contribution to the Theory of Economic Growth," *Quarterly Journal of Economics* 70, no. 1 (1956): 65–94, http://www.jstor.org/stable/1884513.

The *Final* sheet also mentions Trevor Swan's paper, published later in the same year: T. Swan, "Economic Growth and Capital Accumulation," *Economic Record* 32, no. 63 (1956): 334–61. In this paper, which gave rise to the term "Solow–Swan Model," Swan tries to "put up a scarecrow (as Joan Robinson calls it) to keep off the index-number birds and Joan Robinson herself" (343). Swan says, "Capital is made up of a large number of identical meccano [erector] sets which never wear out and can be put together, taken apart, and reassembled with negligible cost or delay in a great variety of models so as to work with various combinations of Labour and Land" (344). Economists quickly gave up the pretense of trying to defend the model from the index-number birds and simply assumed them away.

Novales, A., E. Fernández, and J. Ruíz 2009. *Economic Growth: Theory and Numerical Solution Methods*. Springer.

3.3

The Golden Rule: *GoldenRule.xls*

My best known paper of the period, on the "golden rule"
of national saving, grew out of the industry of research on
growth paths started by Solow's famous paper.
– Edmund Phelps

Quick Summary

To access *GoldenRule.xls*, visit

http://www.depauw.edu/learn/macroexcel/excelworkbooks/SolowModel/
GoldenRule.xls

GoldenRule.xls builds on *KAcc.xls*, with special focus on comparative statics, including transitional dynamics. As with all of the workbooks in the Solow Model series, the *EqPath* sheet enables quick simulation to reveal clearly the steady-state solution and perform sophisticated comparative statics analyses.

Screencasts

- http://vimeo.com/econexcel/grcs: uses the canonical graph (Solow diagram) to do comparative statics
- http://vimeo.com/econexcel/groptimals: uses graphs and *Solver* to find the saving rate that maximizes *c*
- http://vimeo.com/econexcel/grnameexplained: demonstrates the temporary decrease in *c* after increasing *s* to its Golden Rule value; uses the ⟨Comp Statics⟩ button

Introduction

Before extending the basic model in *KAcc.xls* with population growth and technological progress, this workbook explores an especially interesting comparative statics analysis that has come to be known as the Golden Rule. Previously, we merely examined how changes in the saving rate, *s*, affect steady-state values of the endogenous variables; now the idea is to have policy makers find the optimal *s*, that is, that saving rate that maximizes steady-state consumption. The fact that the optimal saving rate is called the Golden Rule saving rate is usually explained via the canonical Solow diagram, but there is a better way – simulation and direct observation of the results. The canonical graph makes the comparison between steady-states clear, but it requires exceedingly careful reading to extract the path taken from the initial to the new steady-state. Via simulation, the transitional dynamics that make attaining the Golden Rule difficult can be clearly highlighted.

Common Problems for Students

Without a doubt, the two biggest problems for students are the term *Golden Rule* and the introduction of an optimization problem into an equilibrium model. Both are best handled by clearly explaining, up front, exactly what is going on.

Although there are many versions of the Golden Rule, a common statement is "do unto others as you would have them do unto you." In a classic paper, Phelps (1961, 642) applied this ethic of reciprocity across generations in a Solow Model:

In a golden age [i.e., steady-state] governed by the golden rule, each generation invests on behalf of future generations that share of income which, subject to [the investment function], it would have had past generations invest on behalf of it. We have shown that, among golden-age paths of natural growth, that golden age is best which practices the golden rule.

Phelps (1965, 793) credits Allais, Desrousseaux, Robinson, and Swan as precursors, but there is little doubt that he was responsible for popularizing the concept. By focusing on each generation's responsibility to future generations, Phelps used the model in a novel way and sparked a policy debate about the saving rate. *GoldenRule.xls* can be used to demonstrate how a present generation must forgo consumption when the saving rate is increased to the optimal *s*. That the present generation sacrifices for future generations because that is what the present generation would have wanted done for them is why it is called the Golden Rule. Explicitly describing the present generation acting as it would wish other generations would have acted changes the Golden Rule from an abstract idea in the minds of students to a clear, well-named concept.

Overlaying an optimization problem over an equilibrium model makes sense once one realizes that the saving rate can be influenced by tax policy and other incentives. We define an agent (the government or policy maker) with an optimization problem and show how steady-state consumption is a

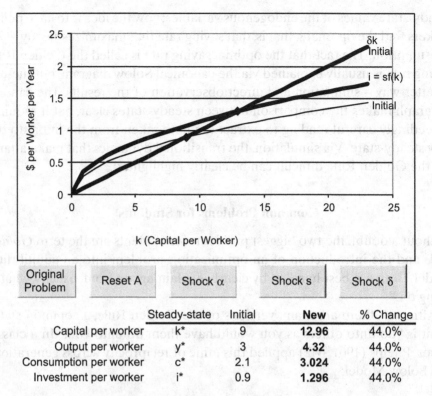

Figure 3.3.1. Using the canonical graph for comparative statics exercises.

Source: GoldenRule sheet in *GoldenRule.xls* after clicking the   Shock A   button.

function of *s*. This makes clear the separation between an equilibrium model and an optimization problem.

Defining terms clearly and providing a road map for your audience are best-practice lecturing techniques that are especially needed when teaching the Golden Rule. The material is difficult enough that taking the time up front to prepare a good foundation is worth the effort.

The *CS* Sheet

To teach the Golden Rule effectively, it is best to begin by reviewing the comparative statics properties of the model. The *CS* sheet makes this painless. Click on the buttons below the canonical solution graph (see Figure 3.3.1) to display the appropriate shift and new optimal solution. The buttons, such as   Shock A , simply change one of the parameters in cells B5:B8, which causes the chart to update. For example, clicking the button (as was done in Figure 3.3.1) changes cell B5 from 1 to 1.2. The initial solution values for the four variables are displayed, along with the new solution values and corresponding percentage changes.

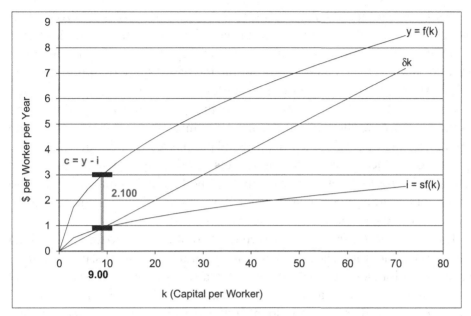

Figure 3.3.2. Using the canonical graph to find the Golden Rule saving rate. *Source: GoldenRule* sheet in *GoldenRule.xls.*

In a lecture or as homework, one can use parameter values other than the ones produced by the buttons under the chart. Simply enter the desired value in cells B5:B8. Use the $\boxed{\substack{\text{Unlock Y} \\ \text{Axis}}}$ button if the solution is off the chart (e.g., when $A = 2$). To generate a decrease in k^*, directly enter an appropriate shock. For example, 0.2 in cell B7 will cause the saving rate to fall and the investment function to shift down.

This sheet should be used to make clear that the saving rate will influence the steady-state values of k, y, c, and i. When the saving rate is increased, the investment function shifts up, thereby producing a higher steady-state k (at the intersection of the new investment and δk functions). But we are not interested in k or even y because the measure we seek to maximize is consumption per worker. To show this on the canonical graph, we need a new curve, which is exactly what the next sheet, *GoldenRule*, does.

The *GoldenRule* Sheet

With an understanding of how shocks in the exogenous variables affect the steady-state solution, we are ready to find the Golden Rule saving rate. The canonical graph in the *GoldenRule* sheet has been augmented with $y = f(k)$ so that the difference between the y and i functions is consumption per worker, as shown in Figure 3.3.2.

The scroll bar on cell E7 can be used to change *s* in cell B7. It is obvious that as *s* rises toward 50%, steady-state consumption rises; but beyond this point, although steady-state *y* continues to rise, steady-state *c* falls. Increases in *s* produce more *y*, which increases *c*, but the increased share of output devoted to investment lowers *c*. The optimal trade-off of these effects occurs when $s = \alpha$, as Phelps (1961) showed, which is the answer to the question posed in the *GoldenRule* sheet about this model's "interesting property." Thus, the optimal saving rate is 50% for the original parameter values. Click the Rand button to produce different parameter sets (for display in class or assigned as a task in the *ToDo* sheet). Knowing that optimal *s* equals *α* makes it simple to check student homework answers and allows instant identification of optimal *s* when producing random parameter values while lecturing.

The *GoldenRule.xls* workbook includes two other ways to find the optimal saving rate. The *Math* sheet, not mentioned in the screencasts, uses the first-order condition, setting the derivative of steady-state *c* with respect to *s* equal to zero, to find the optimal solution. Click the Show Math button near cell I1 of the *EqPath* sheet to display the hidden *Math* sheet. In addition, Excel's *Solver* can also be used to find optimal *s*. *Solver* is an Excel add-in that is in the **Data** tab (or in the **Tools** menu in Excel 2003 or earlier). If it is not listed, use the Add-Ins Manager to install it. The workbook is prepared such that the target and changing cells are already filled in when *Solver* is called. Simply click **Solve** in the *Solver* dialog box to find the optimal solution. The http://vimeo.com/econexcel/groptimals screencast demonstrates how to use *Solver* to find optimal *s*.

The *EqPath* Sheet

Having explained that the Golden Rule *s* is the value that maximizes consumption per worker, the next and final step is to justify a claim: this is one of the best-named phenomena in all of economics. Usually, we are frustrated by a confusing nomenclature that mixes plain words with technical meaning (e.g., investment or efficiency) or credits the wrong person with a concept – this is a really long list, but my favorite example is from Blaug (1997, 523): "Irving Fisher did not invent the Ideal Index Number and actually pleaded (in vain) that it should not be named after him." The Golden Rule, however, delivers exactly what is needed – it is catchy, different, and gives away its meaning.

Teaching the concept of the Golden Rule is best accomplished by abandoning the Solow diagram and using simulated time paths of consumption per worker. As the screencast http://vimeo.com/econexcel/grnameexplained shows, the Comp Statics button makes it easy to chart *c* over time, before and after moving to optimal *s*. This button allows the user to run the economy for any combination of parameter values for as long as indicated and then

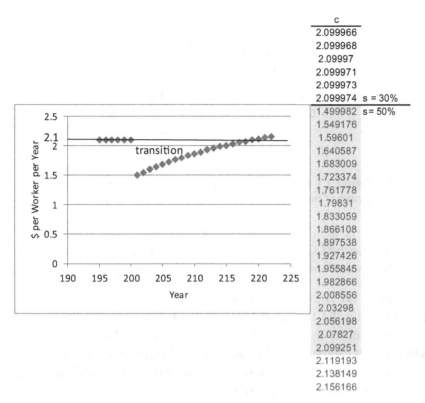

c	
2.099966	
2.099968	
2.09997	
2.099971	
2.099973	
2.099974	s = 30%
1.499982	s = 50%
1.549176	
1.59601	
1.640587	
1.683009	
1.723374	
1.761778	
1.79831	
1.833059	
1.866108	
1.897538	
1.927426	
1.955845	
1.982866	
2.008556	
2.03298	
2.056198	
2.07827	
2.099251	
2.119193	
2.138149	
2.156166	

Figure 3.3.3. Explaining why it is called the Golden Rule by directly examining *c*. *Source: Fig 333* (hidden) sheet in *GoldenRule.xls*.

allows the user to change a single exogenous variable and run the economy again. For the initial parameter values, the data are deadened (the cells contain numbers, not formulas) and, therefore, remain constant as the exogenous variables change. For the new parameter values, however, the data are based on formulas that respond to any changes in cells B5:B8. This enables the simulation to show transitional dynamics for any shock or shocks.

As shown in Figure 3.3.3 (unhide the *Fig 333* sheet to use this chart), plotting the data around the transition period provides a striking visual of the Golden Rule that can be used to teach the concept effectively. It is plainly clear that the people living through the transition from $s = 30\%$ to 50% suffer a decrease in c from years 201 to 219 (when $c < 2.1$). This can be teased out of the canonical graph by carefully displaying the difference between y and i, but such gymnastics are best suited for teaching the Solow Model at a level beyond the needs of most undergraduates.

Figure 3.3.3 is a testament to the ability of simulation to clarify and make a concept accessible. It can also lead to further explorations. Consider these three proposals, generated by students during class discussion, for taking the economy from $s = 30\%$ to its Golden Rule value of 50%:

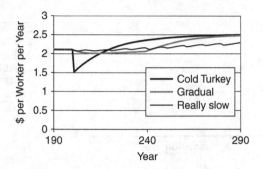

Figure 3.3.4. Transitions under three alternative policies.
Source: Gradual (hidden) sheet in *GoldenRule.xls.*

1. Cold turkey: the usual immediate, one-time shock in *s* from 30% to 50%
2. Gradual: *s* rises by 1% point every other year until it reaches 50%
3. Really slow: *s* rises every ten years but 1% point until it reaches 50%

Unhide the sheet *Gradual* in *GoldenRule.xls* to see how simulation can be used to evaluate the three alternatives. Figure 3.3.4 shows the behavior of the economy under the three alternatives. It is clear that gradualism avoids the cratering of *c* experienced under cold turkey, but it takes much longer to reach maximum *c* in the steady-state. In essence, we are considering alternative trade-offs of future and present consumption.

Whether this is interesting is not the point. Consider instead how simulation enhances creativity and gives students the freedom to explore the model. Many other imaginative questions can be asked and answered using the base platform in the *EqPath* sheet. It is easy to copy the sheet, and it can be modified and extended to handle tweaks to the model.

An easy way to create novelty is by clicking the [Rand] button to create new parameter sets instantly. You and your students can generate additional examples repeatedly. This is demonstrated in the screencast http://vimeo .com/econexcel/grnameexplained and used as a task in the *ToDo* sheet. The $s = \alpha$ shortcut, which the screencast does not reveal, is useful when working with random parameter sets. Sharing this property of the model is not helpful because the student who is unable to understand the optimal saving rate uses it as a rote rule to avoid dealing with the model.

Dynamic inefficiency (generated by starting from a saving rate greater than the optimal *s*) is mentioned in the screencast but not defined or explained in any detail. See Novales et al. (2009, 82) for a careful treatment of dynamic inefficiency and for more on the *Final* sheet's suggestion of discounting consumption flows over time.

Although not covered in the screencast, the time path analysis approach (via the [Comp Statics] button) can be applied to any of the exogenous variables. It can also be used to change *s* from and to any value (not necessarily its optimal value). Such applications would be suitable for extra homework or exam questions. If you have a favorite parameter set or want to replicate an example from a book, copy the *EqPath* sheet and rename it as needed. Enter the desired parameters in range B5:B8 and click the Set Base button to make these values the new base case.

Tasks

The tasks in the *ToDo* sheet follow the structure used for the three screen-casts. The first two tasks explore the effect of a shock in δ via the canonical graph and ask the student to compute the α elasticity of steady-state y, which is $\%\Delta y/\%\Delta\alpha = 73.2\%/20\% \approx 3.66$, so steady-state y is quite responsive to changes in α. The screencast briefly mentions elasticity, so this concept may need to be reviewed.

The next task is based on the second screencast on finding the Golden Rule saving rate and contains four questions. The student uses the Rand button to find optimal s for his or her particular economy using the scroll bar and *Solver*. Obviously, each student will have a different answer, which can be quickly graded via the $s = \alpha$ shortcut. Task 3D forces the student to realize that the two approaches, manually choosing s with the scroll bar and using *Solver*, must give substantially the same answer (*Solver* false precision means they may not be exactly the same) because they are simply alternative ways of solving the exact same problem.

The last task uses the random parameter values from the previous questions in two ways. In task 4A, the student is asked to connect the solutions provided via the canonical graph (in the *GoldenRule* sheet) to the simulation method in the *EqPath* sheet. In task 4B, the student replicates the comparative statics path analysis demonstrated in the screencast and explains why it is called the Golden Rule. This last question may be the most important since it requires an explanation of the Golden Rule.

These tasks closely mirror the material in the screencasts. There is ample room for more questions and novel applications with this workbook, especially using the Rand and Comp Statics buttons in the *EqPath* sheet. As with the screencasts, none of the tasks uses mathematics, which is another potential source of content for courses with appropriate math prerequisites.

Conclusion

The IGM Economic Experts panel "explores the extent to which economists agree or disagree on major public policy issues" (http://www.igmchicago.org). Results from a poll posted on July 8, 2013, show that economists are in substantial agreement on the importance of the saving rate as a determinant of economic growth. When asked their opinion of the following statement that "sustained tax and spending policies that boost consumption in ways that reduce the saving rate are likely to lower long-run living standards," 64% agreed or strongly agreed, 18% were uncertain, and 8% had no opinion. No one disagreed or strongly disagreed (http://tiny.cc/igmsavingrate).

The power of simulation and live graphs in a spreadsheet is on display in the *GoldenRule.xls* workbook. By plotting time paths before and after the move from an initial to optimal *s*, a concrete presentation with strong visuals can be used to explain the Golden Rule and why it is so aptly named. The ⟨ Rand ⟩ button enables endless practice and additional homework or exam questions. The next workbook in the Solow Model series, *Population.xls*, extends the model by adding population growth.

Sources and Further Reading

The epigraph is from Phelps's autobiographical chapter "A Life in Economics," in *The Makers of Modern Economics*, vol. 2, ed. A. Heertje (Edward Elgar, 1995), 92.

Blaug, M. 1997. *Economic Theory in Retrospect*, 5th ed. Cambridge University Press.

IGM Forum. 2013. Homepage. http://www.igmchicago.org. The poll on the saving rate is available at tiny.cc/igmsavingrate. The statements presented to the panel are wide ranging (e.g., minimum wage, bailouts, budget), and it would be a fun learning experience to poll a class and compare results with the experts.

Novales, A., E. Fernández, and J. Ruíz. 2009. *Economic Growth: Theory and Numerical Solution Methods*. Springer.

Phelps, E. 1961. "The Golden Rule of Accumulation: A Fable for Growthmen." *American Economic Review* 51, no. 4: 638–43. http://www.jstor.org/stable/1884513.

Phelps, E. 1965. "Second Essay on the Golden Rule of Accumulation." *American Economic Review* 55, no. 4: 793–814. http://www.jstor.org/stable/1823937.

3.4

Population Growth: *Population.xls*

> In 1830, no general work in economics would omit a
> discussion of population, and in 1930, hardly any general
> work said anything about population.
> – George Stigler

Quick Summary

To access *Population.xls*, visit

http://www.depauw.edu/learn/macroexcel/excelworkbooks/SolowModel/
Population.xls

Population.xls extends the basic model used in *KAcc.xls* and *GoldenRule.xls* by adding population growth. The basic framework remains the same, so the canonical graph is used again and the *EqPath* sheet continues to offer quick simulation to reveal clearly the steady-state solution and perform sophisticated comparative statics analyses. The workbook also contains data on population from three sources, including direct access (from within Excel) to a website with international data from the U.S. Census Bureau.

Screencasts

- http://vimeo.com/econexcel/popworld: world population growth since 1950 and log scale to show it has not grown at a constant rate
- http://vimeo.com/econexcel/popvariouscountries: population growth in various countries with log scale to show differences in growth; effect of European conquest on indigenous peoples
- http://vimeo.com/econexcel/popmalthus: data on England's population; direct editing of SERIES formula to modify a chart
- http://vimeo.com/econexcel/poppyramid: creating a population pyramid chart by accessing U.S. Census data directly from within Excel; animating chart; sex ratio at birth

- http://vimeo.com/econexcel/popproject: forecasting via extrapolation; **PivotTable** to do a cohort component projection (including how the population pyramid chart is made); conditional formatting; discussion of carrying capacity
- http://vimeo.com/econexcel/popsolowmodel: steady-state solution via simulation and comparative statics using the **Scenario Manager**
- http://vimeo.com/econexcel/popfastslown: exploring the ratio of output per worker in two countries with different n, ceteris paribus
- http://vimeo.com/econexcel/popgoldenrulepopgrowth: the Golden Rule in the Solow Model with $n > 0$
- http://vimeo.com/econexcel/popconvergence: speed of convergence and half-life via Excel's MATCH function

Introduction

The basic model in *KAcc.xls* showed that capital accumulation produces growth while catching up to the steady-state but cannot explain the persistent growth in real GDP per person enjoyed by some countries over the last few hundred years. *Population.xls*, the basic model with positive population growth, will show that differences in population growth can explain some of the variation in real GDP per person observed across countries.

When a constant population growth rate parameter, n, is added to the model, the canonical graph retains its basic look and feel, but now the intersection of $(n + \delta)k$ (instead of simply δk) and $sf(k)$ yields the steady-state solution. In essence, capital per worker is eroded by two factors: depreciation of machinery (as before) lowering the numerator and the new effect of a steadily rising number of workers increasing the denominator.

Although the model remains theoretical in nature and no attempt will be made to calibrate it with real-world parameter values, incorporating population growth into the model leads inevitably to discussion of demographics. The *Population.xls* workbook contains data to compute population growth rates and allows the user to compare countries. It also enables direct downloading of single-year cohort data from the International Data Base (IDB) website to display and animate population pyramids in Excel.

The distinction between workers and people offers an avenue for extending the model. The simplifying assumption that all people are workers is maintained throughout. It would be a challenging project for a student to incorporate the labor force participation rate into the Excel workbook. Data on population and labor force are readily available for many countries at http://www.ilo.org.

Common Problems for Students

Extending the model by adding population growth complicates the laws of motion of the system. Dividing by a constant labor force, L, is uncomplicated and does not require a time subscript on the variable. Once we add population growth, we must keep track of the time period by using L_t, where t indicates the time period. While a case can be made for ignoring these details, the opposite alternative is chosen here, and a careful, exactly correct, discrete-time version of the model is presented in the *Algebra* sheet of the *Population .xls* workbook.

A second problem arises from the fact that discussing demographics takes attention away from the mechanics of the model and creates questions that are not answered by the model, since n is constant and exogenous. A decision must be made regarding how deeply to cover population trends and issues. The typical economics student will know very little about demography and is unlikely to encounter it in today's undergraduate curriculum. Thus, spending time on a few facts and acquainting students with the population pyramid (age structure graph) seems optimal.

At the very least, students should know that there is variability in population growth, both over time and across countries. An annual population growth rate of 1% per year is fast, relative to long-run historical experience. Although it was not constant, the rate of growth of world population in the second half of the twentieth century was 1.77% per year. This spectacularly fast growth is unprecedented in all of human history – and completely unforeseen. The United States's population grew rapidly at about 1.3% per year during the twentieth century and is projected to grow more slowly in this century, under 1% per year. Western European countries, conversely, are expected to have the same number of people a few decades from now as they do today. Japan's population will actually decline. Most forecasts have world population peaking this century. However, all of these estimates have a large forecast error, and projecting population for developing countries is even more uncertain. In addition to exposing students to basic facts about population growth, teaching the population pyramid gives students practice reading a chart and opens discussion about many interesting issues, such as male–female ratios by age and dependency ratios.

Demographics

The *Population.xls* workbook uses three data sources from which to deliver a few basic facts about population growth. The data are in hidden sheets, which are revealed by clicking the Show Sheets button in the *Demography* sheet. The first source is population data from the *MaddisonData.xls* workbook. The *Population* sheet has data all the way back to 1 CE for many countries and projects population in 2030. The *Compare* sheet enables informative juxtaposition of countries, display with a log scale, and calculation of growth rates. Second, the *Eng* sheet has annual population data on England from 1541 to 1871 from Wrigley and Schofield (1981). The IDB from the U.S. Census

Bureau is the final source. Without a browser, within Excel (using the *PopPyr* sheet), data are downloaded from the IDB and displayed in a population pyramid that can be animated and copied (for comparisons with other countries). The *5YrPopPyr* sheet allows quick perusal of pyramids in five-year groupings for all countries.

There is easily enough material in these sheets for an entire class period. Most students have not seen a population pyramid chart and therefore it requires careful presentation. One great advantage of spending time on population data is that the mathematical tools used to analyze growth in real GDP per person are used again, providing much needed repetition and practice.

Demography Screencasts and Tasks

The screencasts and associated tasks in the *ToDo* sheet are organized into five areas: (1) world population, (2) individual countries, (3) England and Malthus, (4) population pyramid, and (5) forecasting. Tasks 1, 2, and 5 have concealed answer sheets that can be displayed by running the *ToggleHide-Unhide* macro using any of these three methods: (1) from the **Developer** tab, click **Macros**, or (2) press ALT-F8 and select the *ToggleHideUnhide* macro and click **Run**, or (3) use the keyboard shortcut CTRL-SHIFT-U.

World Population

In this screencast, the *Compare* sheet is used to chart world population from 1950 to 2000 and the compound annual growth rate (CAGR) of 1.77% per annum is shown. World population from 1 CE to the present is then displayed, and the tremendous increase in population since World War II is emphasized. A log scale is used to dramatically demonstrate that world population did not grow at a constant rate. The task follows up on this point, asking the student to compute annual percentage changes from 1950 to 2009, chart the results, and report the maximum value. It was 2.13% in 1971, which is a ridiculously fast world population growth rate.

Individual Countries

Again using the *Compare* sheet, in this screencast the population of the United States over time is charted and then compared to Mexico, which is growing much faster. Again, a log scale is used for better analysis – Mexico's faster growth is hard to see in natural units and easy to see with a log scale. Task 2B asks when Mexico would surpass the United States if growth rates remained constant. The answer is 2099, and the work can be seen by revealing the *ToDo2* sheet (with keyboard shortcut CTLR-SHIFT-U), which also has the answers to the other questions. The screencast points out that, once a log scale is used, the data clearly show the extremely unfortunate effects of the European conquest on indigenous peoples around the globe. Population in Germany, France, Italy, and the United Kingdom since 1950 are compared, followed by the two most populous countries in the world, China and India. Linear and log scales are used in each case. In a final comparison between Cuba and the Dominican Republic, the log scale is touted as offering a "special set of glasses" for data analysis.

England and Malthus

This screencast opens by defining Malthusianism and explains why Malthus (1798) was interested in population. It is in fact true that England was growing faster than it had been. Data from Wrigley and Schofield (1981) in the *Eng* sheet make that plainly clear. The screencast takes an Excel aside and demonstrates how to place a marker on a graph by directly entering numbers into the SERIES formula. It then uses http://econlib.org to chase down the source of Malthus's (1798, II.7) claim "that population, when unchecked, goes on doubling itself every twenty-five years." Smith ([1776] 1904) has the exact same estimate, and a Google search finds Smith's source in Mitchell (1767, 22).

The answer to task 3A is in cells A402 and B402 of the *Eng* sheet. The answer to task 3B is that the two growth rates are not similar. England is growing almost twice as fast as the United Kingdom (and we are ignoring that England is part of the United Kingdom). Perhaps there is some truth in Smith's ([1776] 1904, I.8.23) statement that "the most decisive mark of the prosperity of any country is the increase of the number of its inhabitants."

Population Pyramid

The screencast walks the student through downloading single-year age cohort data from the IDB website from within the *PopPyr* sheet. This is a rich resource that is simple to use and leads to many interesting questions. After a pyramid for the United States for 2012 (see Figure 3.4.1) is created, multiple years of data are downloaded for Japan, and the pyramid is animated.

The last example is China, which can be used to explore a variety of issues. Male–female sex ratios are computed and the marked preference for boys in China is easily seen. The screencast concludes by scrolling through the *5YrPopPyr* sheet, which makes clear the diversity of pyramids. This sheet can be used to identify particular countries for additional assignments or further exploration. Unhide the *IDBYearsAvail* sheet to see the data availability for each country.

Usage notes explaining how to use the buttons under the chart are in column Q. One caveat is that the IDB website can be quite slow, especially when

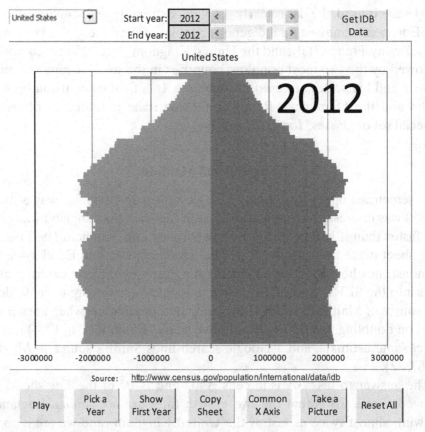

Figure 3.4.1. Population pyramid.
Source: PopPyr sheet (revealed from *Demography* sheet) in *Population.xls*.

several users hit it at once. This can pose a problem for class or lab work. Downloading only one year (instead of many) or staggering when students try to download the data are options. The actual Excel work is trivial – once the data are loaded, the macro runs almost instantaneously. If you experience delays, it is almost surely due to slow download. For a presentation, you can always download the data beforehand, copy the sheet, and save the workbook. Also, the chart itself is quite large, so use Excel's zoom control if needed to fit the entire chart on-screen.

Run the macro *MakePopPyrAlone* (from the **Developer** tab, click **Macros** or press ALT-F8) to create a workbook that has only the *PopPyr* and *5YrPopPyr* sheets (and all supporting Visual Basic code). Note that running this macro will save the existing *Population.xls* workbook, delete all other sheets in the workbook, including any pyramids you have created, and then save the workbook as *PopulationPyramid.xls* in the current folder. This workbook can be used for other courses or presentations where the other sheets are not needed.

Forecasting

A fundamental message is that population projections are exceedingly difficult. There are two basic approaches, extrapolation and modeling. The simplest type of extrapolation is demonstrated with Excel using world population. The cohort component method is outlined using world five-year cohort
data in the *5YrPopPyr* sheet. An Excel **PivotTable** is created and the data
are charted as a bar graph with options set to 100% series overlap and no
gap width. Modeling is briefly described and conditional formatting is used
on Maddison's forecasts in the *Population* sheet. This long screencast (12:44)
concludes with a brief discussion of carrying capacity, emphasizing the uncertainty in determining how many people the planet can hold.

Of course, the demography covered barely scratches the surface. For
more content, Cohen (1995) and Weil (2013) offer many additional demo-
graphic facts and charts. The former makes repeated reference to the United
Nations's projections of world population made in 1992 (see Cohen 1995,
141), which can be checked with IDB data. The latter's Chapter 5, *Future
Population Trends*, offers several charts that can be replicated with IDB
data, such as the fraction of working-age Americans over time (Weil 2013,
141).

The Solow Model with Population Growth

Having introduced a few fundamental ideas from demography, we are ready
to return to the Solow Model and augment it with constant population
growth. Analytically, there is little new. Population growth works much the
same as depreciation, diluting the available machinery per worker. At the
steady-state, the equilibrium condition becomes

$$\Delta k = sAk_t^\alpha - (\delta + n)k_t = 0.$$

Solving for k yields the steady-state solution

$$k^* = \left(\frac{sA}{\delta + n}\right)^{1/1-\alpha}.$$

As before, once steady-state k is determined, steady-state y, c, and i and the
level versions of all of the variables can be found simply by evaluating the
variables at steady-state k.

Unfortunately, to get the time path exactly right in the Excel implementation of this discretized process, a $(1 + n)$ term is needed. Explaining this
$(1 + n)$ term requires algebra.

To Do or Not to Do Algebra?

The *Algebra* sheet (unhidden after clicking the [Show Algebra] button on cell I1 in the *EqPath* sheet) in *Population.xls* lays out in painstaking detail the equations of the model. This can be skipped, but it is not really that difficult, although it admittedly requires a level of attention beyond the reach of some under-graduate students. One virtue is that the student is exposed to yet another way of interacting with the model. In addition, the algebra makes clear why the change in k formula in column H of the *EqPath* sheet has been modified from the previous workbooks, dividing Δk by $(1 + n)$.

Many texts take an intermediate approach. For example, Mankiw (2013, 232) offers a few equations in a footnote, which concludes, "After a bit of manipulation, this produces the equation $[\Delta k = i - (\delta + n)k]$ in the text." Too many steps are skipped, however, in that "bit of manipulation," and little understanding is gained. Either go over the steps in the *Algebra* sheet with some care or skip it entirely. The *Algebra* sheet has enough detailed, step-by-step explanation that it can be assigned as independent work to those interested in understanding the finer points of the model.

The exposition in the *Algebra* sheet tries to offer an intellectual pat on the back for the student who perseveres to the end by saying that the con-ventional approach, simply positing the steady-state condition, sweeps all of this under the rug. The *Algebra* sheet concludes with, "Now you know what is really going on in the Solow Model with population growth, instead of merely memorizing a steady-state equation without understanding it."

By doing the algebra, you can explicitly show how n appears in the steady-state condition (starting at row 111 in the *Algebra* sheet). It is true that pop-ulation growth acts like depreciation by decreasing capital per worker, but the channel is different. Depreciation wears away capital, while population growth lowers capital per worker by spreading capital over more workers.

To be clear, following the algebra is not going to make your students experts with the Solow Model. The polar opposite approach of simply stat-ing that $\Delta k = sy - (\delta + n)k$ seems worse because it magically introduces n without adequate explanation. For those who disagree and worry students will be lost or terrified by the algebraic manipulations, skipping this content does not preclude using the rest of the workbook.

EqPath Screencasts and Tasks

The first screencast reviews the mechanics of the model quickly and finds the initial steady-state solution. The majority of the time is spent on using Excel's *Scenario Manager* to do comparative statics, showing that the steady-state is negatively impacted by increases in n. Comparative statics via the

Solow diagram is straightforward (simply rotate the $(\delta + n)k$ function counterclockwise as n rises) and left as a task, which utilizes the Rand button to create individualized problems for each student. The analytical work is clear-cut, with $k^* = (sA/(\delta + n))^{1/1-\alpha}$ and, from the production function, $y^* = A(sA/(\delta + n))^{\alpha/1-\alpha}$.

The next screencast explores output per worker in two countries that are the same in every respect, except population growth. It charts y in both countries over time (directly editing the SERIES formula) and shows that the low population growth country enjoys a higher output per worker throughout its time path. This is the signature result of the Solow Model with population growth. For the mathematically inclined, task 7B has the student form the ratio

$$\frac{y^*_{\text{low }n}}{y^*_{\text{high }n}} = \frac{A\left(\frac{sA}{\delta + n_{\text{low}}}\right)^{\alpha/1-\alpha}}{A\left(\frac{sA}{\delta + n_{\text{high}}}\right)^{\alpha/1-\alpha}} = \left(\frac{\delta + n_{\text{low}}}{\delta + n_{\text{high}}}\right)^{-\alpha/1-\alpha} = \left(\frac{\delta + n_{\text{high}}}{\delta + n_{\text{low}}}\right)^{\alpha/1-\alpha}.$$

With this analytical expression for the ratio of steady-state y in the low- and high-n countries, the answer for any parameter set used in task 7A can be quickly graded. For example, evaluated at the parameters for the original problem compared to an economy with $n = 2\%$, we find that steady-state y will be 9% higher in the original economy (with $n = 1\%$):

$$\frac{y^*_{\text{low }n}}{y^*_{\text{high }n}} = \left(\frac{\delta + n_{\text{high}}}{\delta + n_{\text{low}}}\right)^{\alpha/1-\alpha} = \left(\frac{0.1 + 0.02}{0.1 + 0.01}\right)^{0.5/1-0.5} = {}^{0.12}/_{0.11} \approx 1.09.$$

The answer for task 7C is that the analytical expression for the ratio of steady-state y shows that A and s have no effect on this ratio; however, it is sensitive to changes in n, α, and δ.

In the third screencast, the Golden Rule is reviewed (it is assumed that the student has done the *GoldenRule.xls* workbook) and shown to work the same way with $n > 0$ as before, when we had no population growth. It also remains true that the Golden Rule saving rate equals α in this model, but no mention is made of the result. Excel's *Solver* is used to find the Golden Rule saving rate, and the Comp Statics button is used to demonstrate the decrease in c immediately after the increase in s that gives the Golden Rule its name. Although there is nothing new here, the Golden Rule is a difficult concept, and the repetition is a good way to improve retention. Two tasks are available. The first has the student replicate the screencast with a random parameter set and show that n has no effect on the Golden Rule saving rates (as before, optimal $s = \alpha$), while the second asks if there is a transition issue when n changes. The latter task is difficult because the student has to figure out that the question requires using the Comp Statics button to do an analysis of decreasing n. The answer is that there is no transition issue – the economy smoothly goes (c never falls) from an initial to its new steady-state solution after n is decreased.

The final screencast focuses on the speed of convergence to the steady-state. No mention is made of the Taylor series approximation, $(1 - \alpha)(\delta + n)$, which has become standard fare in the literature (Weiss 2000, 3) because the derivation is too difficult to present to students and it only works reasonably well close to the steady-state. (For a complete explanation, reveal the *Taylor* sheet by unhiding it.) Instead, a simple definition of the speed of convergence is used. For any variable, Z_t, converging to its steady-state solution, Z^*, the gap at any point in time, is $Z^* - Z_t$. Computing $-\frac{(Z^*-Z_{t+1})-(Z^*-Z_t)}{(Z^*-Z_t)}$ is a natural extension of the percentage change that measures how much of the gap is covered, in percentage points, from one time period to the next. Since the gap is becoming smaller in the next period, the minus sign makes the expression positive and easier to communicate when convergence is faster (greater percentage change) and slower (smaller percentage change).

The formula makes clear that the speed of convergence is not simply the percentage change in Z_t, which measures how fast Z_t is changing, but the percentage change in the gap itself. Thus, the speed of convergence depends both on how fast Z_t is moving and how far away it is from Z^*. For the Solow Model, the speed of convergence is sensitive to α, the marginal productivity of capital (and capital per worker), and this is easily shown in the screencast, which demonstrates how to copy a chart as a picture without a background and paste it over an existing, live chart.

The speed of convergence is also viewed in terms of half-life, the time required for half of the gap to be closed. Excel's MATCH function makes it simple to compute the half-life, which is quickly displayed at the end. The task is uncomplicated, replicating the screencast with a random parameter set. Convergence is confusing, so repetition is helpful. The ideas used here will be used again in the Solow Model with technological progress.

Conclusion

Augmenting the model with population growth has two parts: empirical and theoretical. The former requires a decision about how much demography to cover. *Population.xls* uses Maddison's population data to enable students to gain a rough sense of how fast and variably population has grown in different countries over time. The workbook also uses population pyramids to break down total population into age and sex cohorts, using data downloaded directly within Excel from the IDB website.

Adding population to the Solow Model is, in a sense, analytically trivial since we simply include n in the steady-state equation, $\Delta k = sAk_t^\alpha - (\delta + n)k_t = 0$. This, however, masks substantial changes in the mechanics of the discrete-time version of the model. The hidden *Algebra* sheet has the details. The *EqPath* sheet can be used to simulate the economy and show how higher *n*, ceteris paribus, lowers steady-state values of the endogenous variables.

Population.xls, like its predecessor, *KAcc.xls*, fails to generate sustained economic growth, and therefore we must extend the model again. The last workbook in the Solow Model series, *TechProgress.xls*, incorporates technological progress, and this addition produces persistent economic growth.

Sources and Further Reading

The epigraph is from G. Stigler, "The Influence of Events and Policies on Economic Theory,"*American Economic Review* 50, no. 2 (1960): 36, http://www.jstor.org/stable/1815008.

Cohen, J. 1995. *How Many People Can the Earth Support?* W. W. Norton.

Malthus, T. 1798. *An Essay on the Principle of Population*, 1st ed. http://www.econlib.org/library/Malthus/malPop1.html.

Mankiw, N. 2013. *Macroeconomics*. 9th ed. Worth.

Mitchell, J. 1767. *The Present State of Great Britain and North America: With Regard to Agriculture, Population, Trade, and Manufactures, Impartially Considered.* https://books.google.com/books?id=hqsNAAAAQAAJ.

Smith, A. (1776) 1904. *An Inquiry into the Nature and Causes of the Wealth of Nations*. Methuen. http://www.econlib.org/library/Smith/smWN.html.

Weil, D. 2013. *Economic Growth*. 3rd ed. Prentice Hall.

Weiss, J. 2000. "On the Convergence Speed of Growth Models." Working Paper 22/2000, Faculty of Economics and Management Magdeburg (FEMM). http://ssrn.com/abstract=243945.

Wrigley, E., and R. Schofield. 1981. *The Population History of England, 1541–1871*. Edward Arnold.

3.5

Technological Progress: *TechProgress.xls*

> If a series of nuclear explosions were to wipe out the
> material equipment of the world but the educated citizens
> survived, it need not be long before former standards were
> reconstituted; but if it destroyed the educated citizens,
> even though it left the buildings and machines intact, a
> period longer than the Dark Ages might elapse before the
> former position was restored.
> – Lionel Robbins

Quick Summary

To access *TechProgress.xls*, visit

http://www.depauw.edu/learn/macroexcel/excelworkbooks/SolowModel/
TechProgress.xls

TechProgress.xls is the last of the workbooks in the Solow Model series. It
includes population growth and exogenous, constant technological change.
The *EqPath* sheet enables straightforward simulation to reveal clearly the
steady-state solution in both efficiency and own units of per worker variables.
Sophisticated comparative statics analyses, including transitional dynamics,
can be easily performed. Real-world, Maddison data are used to calibrate and
"test" the model. These applications are interesting, enjoyable, and thought
provoking.

Screencasts

- http://vimeo.com/econexcel/techproginitial: introduction stressing imaginary (efficiency units) and real economies
- http://vimeo.com/econexcel/techprogcatchuptheory: catch-up growth and convergence; steady-state path as a magnet

- http://vimeo.com/econexcel/techprogcalibrateusa: Solow Model calibrated to match U.S. economic performance in the twentieth century
- http://vimeo.com/econexcel/techprogcatchupgermany: capital "destroyed" in the *EqPath* sheet and Germany's post–World War II performance replicated
- http://vimeo.com/econexcel/techprograndom: stochastic disturbance term added via NORMALRANDOM(mean, SD)
- http://vimeo.com/econexcel/techprogcompstatics: explores the effects of shocks in n, s, and g on the level and growth rate of steady-state y
- http://vimeo.com/econexcel/techproggoldenrule: the Golden Rule with $g > 0$; as g rises, the transition period gets shorter
- http://vimeo.com/econexcel/techprogconvergence: shows why CAGR as a function of log y is used; shows that the predicted relationship fails for large samples but is better for more similar countries

Introduction

Teaching and learning the Solow Model effectively and comprehensively is hard work. *TechProgress.xls* is the third (and final) step in a progression of models. Starting from the most primitive version of the model presented in *KAcc.xls*, a nonzero, constant rate of population growth was added in *Population.xls*. This changed the steady-state equation (or equilibrium condition) from $\Delta k = s f(k) - \delta k_t = 0$ to $\Delta k = s f(k) - (\delta + n)k_t = 0$. Augmented with population growth, the model shows that increasing n, ceteris paribus, lowers steady-state k, y, c, and i; but once the steady-state is reached, it still does not exhibit persistent economic growth.

For the model to produce the sustained increases in real GDP per person observed in rich countries since the relatively recent arrival of the market system (the last few hundred years), a further extension must be made. By incorporating an exogenous, constant rate of technological progress, g, the model's behavior is different, and persistent growth is generated.

There are learning costs, however. To maintain ties to the earlier versions, technological progress is modeled as labor augmenting, and a new term, *efficiency units*, is born. The steady-state equation becomes $\Delta k = s f(k) - (\delta + n + g)k = 0$, which bears a strong resemblance to the previous versions, except k is now capital per worker in efficiency units.

Although we can keep going, of course, endogenizing g with human capital accumulation, adding utility functions to derive optimal saving, and more, the model with exogenous technological change captures the essence of modern, neoclassical growth theory. Thus, teaching *TechProgress.xls* is an optimal stopping point – not covering this material means not explaining persistent growth, and going beyond this model, while appropriate for a course on growth, seems excessive in time and toil for most intermediate macroeconomics courses.

Common Problems for Students

Adding a positive, constant rate of technological progress to the Solow Model triggers a cascade of difficulties. The laws of motion get more complicated, so the algebra gets harder. The steady-state is now no longer a point, but a path, so convergence becomes trickier. Clever variable transformations into efficiency units enable continued use of the Solow diagram to solve the model, but the transformations are hard to follow and easy to forget. But without a doubt, the most confusing feature of the conventional exposition of the model – and the primary reason for implementing the model in Excel – lies in the comparative statics properties of *g*.

The canonical graph or Solow diagram (Figure 3.1.1) seems to show that n, δ, and g all work the same way: shocks to the model in the form of higher rates of these three variables lower steady-state capital per worker in efficiency units. While true for efficiency units, these shocks do not yield similar results in terms of the actual units of capital per worker. Unlike n and δ, improvements in technological progress help the economy. This is a critical point that must be clearly explained.

To overcome the confusion generated by the Solow Model's use of labor in efficiency units in the canonical graph, the *EqPath* sheet in *TechProgress.xls* clearly separates the simulated economy into imaginary and actual sections. The former represents the economy in efficiency units, while the latter transforms the variables back into their own units. Transforming the variables back into their own units by removing the imaginary workers provides a transparent view of how an increase in the rate of technological progress boosts the real economy. The distinction between imaginary and actual economies is emphasized in the text in the *Tech* sheet and in several screencasts.

Modeling Technological Progress

The *Tech* sheet in *TechProgress.xls* explains labor-augmenting technological change and the key concept of labor in efficiency units (or effective workers). By using a functional form of $Y_t = A_t^{1-\alpha} K_t^\alpha L_t^{1-\alpha}$, we can see that $Y_t = K_t^\alpha (A_t L_t)^{1-\alpha}$. This makes the strategy of treating technological progress as if more workers are available crystal clear. The *Tech* sheet has a series of simple examples where n and g (in yellow-background cells) can be changed to see the effect on population and imaginary workers. It also offers accounting as an illustration to firmly ground the idea of labor-augmenting technological change. Asking for other examples in class might help cement this concept.

Because it is easy to forget (especially if the Solow diagram is the primary mode of exposition), it is important to repeatedly emphasize the notion of imaginary workers as a convenient way to solve the model. With A_t growing at rate g, technological progress acts just like population growth in terms of efficiency units in the model. The *Tech* sheet points out that the number of effective workers grows according to $A_{t+1}L_{t+1} = (1+g)(1+n)A_tL_t$ and posits the steady-state condition as $\Delta k = sf(k) - (\delta + n + g)k = 0$.

As was the case with population growth, deriving this condition requires algebra, which is written out in detail in a hidden sheet, accessible through a button (near the bottom of the *Tech* sheet). Reveal the *Algebra* sheet to see a step-by-step, detailed derivation of the steady-state condition. Not only does the evolution of Δk require a $(1+n)(1+g)$ term in the denominator, it also has an ng term in the numerator, which is often dropped for convenience in standard presentations of the model. The *Algebra* sheet points out that for small rates of population growth and technological progress, ng will be very small. The algebra can be tedious, but it is a good resource for better students. This material can be confidently assigned on an independent study basis because each step is clearly documented.

Introducing the Solow Model with Technological Progress to Students

The opening screencast, available at http://www.vimeo.com/econexcel/techproginitial, begins by reviewing and summarizing previous versions of the Solow Model. This is important because it makes clear to the student the progression from the stripped-down *KAcc.xls* to *GoldenRule.xls* to *Population.xls* and, finally, to *TechProgress.xls*.

The screencast encourages the student to read the *Tech* sheet, which lays out the strategy for incorporating technological progress as labor augmenting. The *Tech* sheet is formatted for printing on two double-sided landscaped pages, which is convenient for use as a handout.

Once the labor-augmenting interpretation of technological progress is explained, the model can be solved with the numerical simulation method that has been used before. The screencast shows, however, that an additional step is needed after the solution is found – transforming the variables from efficiency units back into their own units. This is made clear in the *EqPath* sheet by separating the imaginary from the actual economy.

The task associated with this first screencast goes right to the heart of the efficiency units issue, asking the student to find the steady-state solution for a random set of parameters and then explain the difference between steady-state y in efficiency and own units. The *EqPath* sheet has three charts not mentioned or shown in the screencasts that display the percentage change in y_{eff}, actual Y, and y. As before, in efficiency units, there is no growth in the steady-state, but we clearly see sustained economic growth in the actual output and output per person charts (with Y and y growing at constant rates of $g+n$ and g, respectively, in the steady-state).

The second screencast is devoted to the crucial concept of catch-up growth. Two economies with the same exogenous variables are compared side by side: one starts from the steady-state solution, while the other starts from far away. Strictly speaking, no economy will actually reach its steady-state if it has not started there, but we see that the initially low-k economy grows faster, and we say it catches up to its neighbor. Since they share the same steady-state, it is plain to see that the steady-state path acts like a magnet, attracting any value that is not a steady-state value. The comparison of the two countries is made by directly editing the SERIES formula in a chart and is highlighted by use of a log scale.

This screencast attempts to motivate interest by opening with a question: if an economy starts below its steady-state value, is it doomed always to be behind? This is an excellent question with which to begin a classroom lecture or discussion. The associated task asks how the economy will behave when starting from above the steady-state. The answer – it will grow (if at all) more slowly than at the steady-state until it reaches the steadystate – is apparent once one comprehends the idea of the steady-state as a magnet.

The *EqPath* sheet allows the user to quickly create a new economy by changing parameters. If you use your own parameter set, it is recommended that you copy the *EqPath* sheet and rename it as needed. Once the desired parameters are set in range B3:B8, click the Set Base button to make these values the new base case.

Real-World Data and the Solow Model

The next three screencasts and tasks are devoted to putting the model to work on real-world data. The Maddison data are embedded in the *TechProgress.xls* workbook and are revealed by clicking the Show Data button (near cell U3 of the *EqPath* sheet). The answers to the tasks for these three screencasts are contained in very hidden sheets (not accessible by simply unhiding the sheet) that may be revealed by running the *ToggleHideUnhide* macro (with keyboard shortcut CTRL-SHIFT-U). These real-world applications of the Solow Model are powerful, and your students are likely to react favorably to this material.

The first example uses data on real GDP per person for the United States from 1900 to 2000. Parameters are chosen from Mankiw (2013, 252) and used to find the saving rate. *Solver* is used to find the value of A for the production function that yields real GDP per person in the United States in 1900. The steady-state path for this economy is then charted along with actual U.S. data, producing a striking visual – the Solow Model performs remarkably well (especially after correcting the growth rate from 2% to 1.96%). Of course, all that is really going on is that output is growing at the rate observed in that

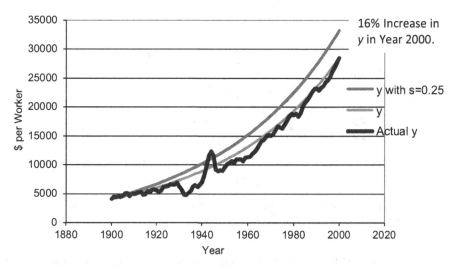

Figure 3.5.1. What if $s = 0.25$ instead of 0.175 for the United States?
Source: ToDo3 sheet in *TechProgress.xls*.

century, so the fit is good by construction, but there is pedagogical value in demonstrating how to calibrate the model.

The associated task has the student replicate the analysis and evaluate how the economy would have performed with a higher saving rate of 25%. The answer is in the *ToDo3* sheet (accessible by keyboard shortcut CTRL-SHIFT-U) and shown in Figure 3.5.1. By the year 2000, output per person would have been 16% higher, according to the Solow Model.

The second screencast in this section is another example of calibration, applying the Solow Model to the case of Germany after World War II. The simulation shows what its economic performance would have been without the war (assuming, unrealistically, that it was and would have stayed on the steady-state path). Plotting actual and steady-state data on the same chart produces an eye-catching result, which is even more surprising when k is "destroyed" (see Figure 3.5.2). The principle of catch-up growth is vividly illustrated and emphasized in the screencast.

The associated task is difficult. The student has to replicate the analysis, change the saving rate to 30%, and evaluate the results. The answer is in the *ToDo4* sheet (accessible by keyboard shortcut CTRL-SHIFT-U) and shown in Figure 3.5.2. While it is true that output per person is unambiguously higher, consumption per person is lower for a few years before taking off. This is, of course, an application of the Golden Rule, but since it is not asked directly, it is difficult to spot.

These two screencasts make no mention of the fact that this version of the Solow Model cannot really explain the economic performance of countries with trade because it is a model of a closed economy. Jones and Romer (2010, 237) point out that, "while the textbook transition dynamics – driven

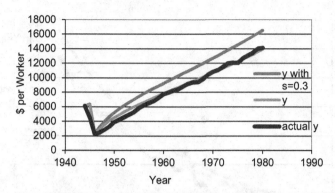

Figure 3.5.2. What if $s = 0.3$ instead of 0.2 after K was destroyed?
Source: ToDo4 sheet in *TechProgress.xls*.

by diminishing returns to capital accumulation – are elegant and easy to explain, they are most likely not especially relevant to catch-up growth in practice." In addition, the calibration approach that was successful for these two countries does not work well for Japan – unhide the sheet *Japan* to see this. These complications are not mentioned in the screencasts, and each professor can decide whether it is worth revealing such issues.

The final screencast in this section returns to the U.S. data and attempts to add randomness to the Solow Model to better reflect observed reality. NORMALRANDOM(mean, SD) is a user-defined function in the *TechProgress.xls* workbook that draws a normally distributed random variable with a given mean and standard deviation (SD). The screencast shows how a stochastic disturbance term can be added to k to produce variability in y over time that roughly matches observed fluctuations in output per person.

The associated task shows that a stochastic term cannot simply be tacked onto y directly because the resulting series looks nothing like observed output per person. The full answer is in the *ToDo5* sheet, revealed by running the *ToggleHideUnhide* macro (with keyboard shortcut CTRL-SHIFT-U). One option not mentioned in the screencast or workbook is to make g stochastic. Instead of using g from cell B3, create a new column with a randomly generated value of g each year and modify the formula in column G to depend on each year's value of g.

There are many ways to incorporate randomness into a Solow Model. Novales et al. (2009) have several Excel workbooks with alternative approaches. They do not use the recalculate (F9) method demonstrated in the screencast, opting instead to put down random numbers in the sheet (e.g., *Dynamic responses.xls* and *Simple simulation.xls*). Replicating their work with the *TechProgress.xls* workbook (along with the Monte Carlo simulation add-in available at http://www.wabash.edu/econometrics) would make for a challenging and interesting advanced independent study or undergraduate thesis.

Comparative Statics with the Solow Model

Three screencasts are devoted to the comparative statics properties of the Solow Model. The first demonstrates a straightforward exploration of the effects of shocks in n, s, and g on the level and growth of steady-state y. Emphasis is placed on the fact that changes in the rate of population growth and saving rates affect the level but not the rate of growth in output per person. The only way to change the rate of growth in steady-state y is by changing g.

The screencast also stresses how increasing g seems to hurt the economy in the canonical graph, which uses efficiency units, but makes clear by comparison of real output per person (in initial and higher g cases) that improving technology helps the economy. The associated task has the student replicate the effect of changing g in efficiency and own units for an economy with a randomly generated parameter set. The *EqPath (2)* sheet that is used in the screencast is hidden in the workbook and can be accessed by simply unhiding it. The screencast makes no mention of the growth rate of y_{eff}, y, and Y charts. You can point out these additional displays and emphasize how the imaginary economy has zero growth, while the actual economy's y grows at g in the steady-state (and actual Y grows at $g + n$).

The second screencast is devoted to the Golden Rule, posing the questions of whether the Golden Rule still operates in a model with technological progress and, if so, how it is affected by $g > 0$. It demonstrates that even in the face of technological progress, the transition period in which present generations sacrifice for future generations remains a part of the model. It is also true, however, that the higher the rate of growth, the shorter the transition and sacrifice.

The screencast uses a hidden sheet, *Zerog* (which can be displayed by unhiding it), to compare the length of transition when $g = 0$ (17 years) to $g = 0.02$ (7 years). With no technological progress, it points out how the imaginary and actual economies are identical since there are no imaginary workers.

The task pushes the logic in the screencast, that higher g means a shorter transition, to an extreme case. By setting $g = 0.4$, the economy grows so quickly that there is, for all practical purposes, no transition period. For the simulation, the numbers displayed by Excel for this fantastically high growth rate are in scientific notation and may require explanation.

The final screencast reviews convergence among countries in theory and practice. By first showing the prediction made by the Solow Model and then examining real-world growth rates, students will understand why the standard graph of growth rates as a function of log y is so popular. In addition, it shows how to use the Excel function NA() to suppress display of data in a chart. There is a lot of material here, and the screencast runs longer than usual, with a length of 12.5 minutes.

The presentation begins by comparing three countries, differing only in initial capital per worker. It is evident that the time paths converge, but further analysis produces an attention-grabbing chart. A plot of CAGR as a function of first-year output per worker for the three countries shows the negative relationship between these two variables. Changing the x-axis to a log scale really makes clear the tight relationship among the three observations.

The scene moves to the *Convergence* sheet, which is Maddison data (from the *PerCapita GDP* sheet), augmented with columns for 1960 real GDP per person and CAGR from 1960 to 2000. A first attempt to create a chart from these two variables fails because Excel is tripped up by calculation errors (e.g., #VALUE! in cell GV24). The solution is to use a dummy variable to create a new series for 1960 real GDP per person. The indicator variable in column GW is 1 if the observation is to be plotted, and 0 if not. The new series is in column GX, and the formula (for the first observation) is = IF(GW5 = 1,GU5.NA()). As the screencast explains, since GW5 = 1, Excel displays 1960 real GDP per person (in cell GU5). For cells with 0 in column GW, the cell evaluates to #N/A. This is useful because charts in Excel do not plot data with #N/A (unlike missing cells, which are treated as zero, or error cells, which we know confuse Excel's charting algorithm). By plotting the cells in column GX (instead of GU) and applying a log scale for the x axis, the chart becomes the standard convergence chart.

The dummy variable and #N/A approach for charting in Excel is exceptionally powerful. It is almost costless to create alternative subsets of observations to be plotted (by creating additional dummy variable columns). The fact that Excel charts simply ignore #N/A data means that #N/A is a convenient way to handle missing data and explains why blank cells in Maddison's original workbook were replaced with #N/A.

Once the standard convergence chart is created, the focus returns to the Solow Model. It is quite clear that we are far away from the prediction of a tight relationship between log initial y and the rate of growth (as demonstrated in the hypothetical, three-country case). The conventional response of focusing on more similar countries is implemented. The screencast shows how simple it is to zero out all of the countries below the United States to focus on high-income countries. An alternative charting strategy is to add a second series with only the high-income countries. This produces Figure 3.5.3, which is also available in the *TechProgress.xls* workbook.

This long screencast ends by emphasizing two related ideas. First, in a large sample of countries, the triangle shape generated by a standard convergence

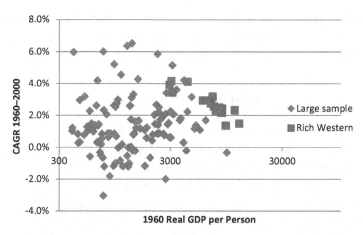

Figure 3.5.3. Convergence in large groups and small subsets of countries. *Source: Convergence* (hidden) sheet in *TechProgress.xls*.

chart (such as Figure 3.5.3) shows that there is great variation at lower initial incomes and much less variation for countries that started off richer. This important point is New Kaldor Fact 3 in Jones and Romer (2010, 236). Second, the Solow Model performs much better when smaller subsets of countries (such as the high-income group in Figure 3.5.3) are examined. This is reinforced at the end of the screencast with a chart displaying strong convergence in U.S. states from Barro and Sala-i-Martin (1992). Updating this with the latest data would be an interesting project. There is a link to their data set at the bottom of the *ToDo* sheet.

The associated task is straightforward – add a fourth country that starts from above steady-state k and determine the effect on the standard convergence chart. This task is made easier because the student clicks a button to reveal the *B*, *C*, and *Convergence* sheets. The answer is that the fourth country lines up exactly with the other three countries and the convergence prediction operates exactly as expected. A more complete answer is in the *ToDo8* sheet, revealed by running the *ToggleHideUnhide* macro (with keyboard shortcut CTRL-SHIFT-U).

One topic not included in the screencast, but potentially useful to show in class or include on an exam, is conditional convergence. Changing an exogenous variable (e.g., n) for one country will produce a new path and, of course, the other two countries will continue converging in their own club, while the third country will not. Note that the growth rate in the steady-state is unaffected by anything other than g, therefore the standard convergence test of CAGR as a function of log initial y remains unchanged.

The *Final* sheet in the workbook, which prints on two landscaped pages, offers a summary of the lessons and weaknesses of the Solow Model. It also points to further work on economic growth models. It requires little effort to modify or supplement the sheet with additional notes or lessons. Unhide the *Future* sheet (or click the button in the *Final* sheet) to access a brief discussion of the debate over the future prospects of growth.

Another Functional Form

Solow (1956) gave three examples of functional forms for the production function. The first was fixed proportions (today also known as Leontief), which he used to replicate the Harrod–Domar model. The second was Cobb–Douglas, which is, of course, the one that made it into every textbook. Solow's (1956, 77) third example is quite interesting: "A whole family of constant-returns-to-scale production functions is given by $Y = (aK^p + L^P)^{1/p}$." With $p = \frac{1}{2}$, it can be written as $Y = a^2K + L + 2a\sqrt{KL}$. The per worker version is then $y = a^2k + 1 + 2a\sqrt{k}$, and this is implemented in a hidden sheet called *Example 3*. The relevant text from Solow (1956) describing the properties of the model with this functional form is included in the *Example 3* sheet along with analytical solutions for steady-state $k, y, c,$ and i. The usual simulation methods can be applied to solve the model and perform comparative statics analyses.

There are several potential uses for this functional form. It can be used for student evaluation such as exam questions and additional homework assignments. It offers a different example for a lecture or as a supplement to a textbook. This might also make a nice application for a growth theory course.

Given the propensity of students to memorize and textbook authors to use the exact same Cobb–Douglas functional form, the *Example 3* sheet will force students to reengage with the mechanics and properties of the model. By zeroing out n and g, a version similar to *KAcc.xls* can be recovered. The Golden Rule can be reviewed under various parameter sets and with $g > 0$, the actual and imaginary economies can be reexamined. In essence, everything covered with the Cobb–Douglas functional form can be repeated with the functional form in the *Example 3* sheet. Interesting repetition is an excellent way to teach and learn.

Modeling Technological Progress by Shocking A

There are expositions of the Solow Model that implement technological change by increasing A and shifting the investment function (e.g., Cowen and Tabarrok 2011, 129). This avoids all of the messiness of efficiency units but allows only for a one-time, single-shot improvement in technology. This seems too far removed from reality, where we observe persistent technological change.

One could allow A to grow at a constant rate, but then we cannot solve the model with the usual equilibrium condition. Unhide the sheet *ShockA* to compare the standard, labor-augmenting strategy with modeling A growing at a constant rate. This comparison may help students understand why efficiency units are the way we solve the model. The sheet explains that we can use the capital-labor ratio as an alternative solution strategy. This approach is much more direct and can be easily utilized on a wide variety of production functions.

Conclusion

This section added technological progress, completing the usual presentation of the Solow Model for an undergraduate audience. In fact, the content is quite conventional, and it was chopped into the usual small pieces for better digestion. Starting with emphasis on capital accumulation and the Golden Rule, population growth was added, and, finally, technological progress was incorporated. What is innovative is the delivery of the model via simulation in Excel and repeated use of data to help explain the model.

The Solow Model is the core of modern growth theory, and it is impossible to teach macroeconomics today without discussing it. Unfortunately, as conventionally presented, it is beyond the grasp of the vast majority of students. While the mechanics of the model are a challenge, the heart of the difficulty lies with the fundamental, canonical graph (see Figure 3.1.1) that every students knows as the Solow diagram. Once improvement in technology is incorporated, a step that is essential to properly model a modern economy, this graph that so deftly solves the model is not able to convey what is actually happening in the economy. Even worse, it seems to say something incredibly counterintuitive, that is, that faster technological progress hurts economic performance.

There really are only two ways around the inadequacy of the canonical graph to explicate the entire model: rely on mathematically sophisticated students to perform incredible feats of variable transformation or use numerical simulation to demonstrate the properties of the model. The fact that professors rely on the former speaks more about how poorly we teach than any real belief that students are capable of learning the Solow Model as it is conventionally presented. To be clear about the crux of the matter, there is no doubt that a student can be taught that the intersection of an investment function, $sf(k)$, and a ray out of the origin, $(\delta + n + g)k$, yields steady-state k. But with $g > 0$, there is no clear way to explain the outcomes produced by an increase in g to the typical undergraduate without simulation.

By evolving the economy with a spreadsheet, the iterative process underlying the model is revealed. The formulas and values can be followed from one cell to the next, making the connections explicit. There is no need to abandon the Solow diagram. Instead, use simulation to support and explain how it really does identify the steady-state solution. Likewise, the equations that represent the laws of motion that students currently memorize with little understanding can be brought to life by referring to each row as another year and directly observing paths of variables over time.

Simulation is not a panacea. It does not guarantee learning or understanding. The Solow Model remains difficult to teach and learn, even with simulation. It is, in my opinion, necessary, but not sufficient – without simulation, it is almost impossible to deeply learn the model; with it, and a lot of hard work by the professor and student, the model becomes accessible and truly understood.

Sources and Further Reading

The epigraph is from L. Robbins, *The Robbins Report*, Higher Education Report of the Committee appointed by the Prime Minister under the Chairmanship of Lord Robbins, Cmnd. 2154 (London: Her Majesty's Stationery Office, 1963), 205, http://www.educationengland.org.uk/documents/robbins/robbins1963.html.

Barro, R., and X. Sala-i-Martin. 1992. "Convergence." *Journal of Political Economy* 100, no. 2: 223–51, http://www.jstor.org/stable/2138606. Since this seminal paper is often cited by papers on convergence at various political and geographic levels, using it to find "items that cited this item" in JSTOR (or other databases) will produce papers on convergence with examples for the classroom, such as convergence in European states and Japanese prefectures.

Cowen, T., and A. Tabarrok. 2011. *Modern Principles: Macroeconomics*. 2nd ed. Worth.

Jones, C., and P. Romer. 2010. "The New Kaldor Facts: Ideas, Institutions, Population, and Human Capital." *American Economic Journal: Macroeconomics*, 2, no. 1: 224–45, http://www.aeaweb.org/articles.php?doi=10.1257/mac.2.1.224.

Mankiw, N. 2013. *Macroeconomics*. 9th ed. Worth.

Novales, A., E. Fernández, and J. Ruíz. 2009. *Economic Growth: Theory and Numerical Solution Methods*. Springer.

4

Macro Data with FRED in Excel

4.1

Introduction: *FRED.xla*

> Teaching economics is a very big responsibility these days.
> Right now [1983] is an especially difficult time to do a
> good job – particularly in teaching macroeconomics.
> That's partly because the subject itself is in a somewhat
> unsettled state and partly because there's always pressure
> to conform to current ideologies whether left or right,
> whether liberal or conservative.
> – Robert M. Solow

There will always be controversy about content and delivery in teaching economics, but one thing we can all agree on is that we need to incorporate data into a modern macroeconomics course. It is obvious that we want our students to be aware of historical trends and the current economic environment. The days of presenting a time series that has not been updated for several years are long gone. Computers and the Internet have removed the constraint on obtaining and processing the latest measures of economic performance and financial statistics.

The Web offers an embarrassment of riches from which to obtain data. Many professors have favorite sources from blogs, aggregator sites, and government portals, such as BLS.gov, WorldBank.org, Penn World Tables, IMF.org, and GapMinder.org. We bookmark our favored sites and return to them to stay up to date and build examples for lectures and assignments. We share these sites with our students and sometimes create detailed instructions on how to use them.

One major problem with teaching students how to access data from a particular website is that it will not remain constant over time. Web redesigns and changing URLs guarantee that our instructions and handouts will be obsolete almost as fast as they are created. This constant evolution of the Web can also make updating an example or lecture handout a chore.

If several different sites are used, there is something to be said for exposing students to various interfaces, but the fixed costs of learning each site (especially if only occasionally accessed) can be quite high. For the professor who visits a site once a semester, it can be frustrating to have to remember how to navigate a site or figure out a new interface. For the student who has never downloaded data, the process can be challenging and time consuming.

While advanced statistical analysis is not appropriate for the typical intermediate macroeconomics course, we often want students to perform rudimentary computations (such as averaging or differencing) and plot variables over time. Some websites offer such capabilities, but often the data are downloaded and imported into Excel for further processing. Fortunately, many websites offer data packaged into Excel files or readable formats (e.g., comma- or tab-delimited), but it is inefficient to begin the process with a browser when the ending point will be Excel since Excel is perfectly capable of directly accessing the Web.

The FRED Excel add-in offers an approach to data access that is both easy and powerful. Instead of learning how to use a variety of websites and then importing data into Excel, the add-in allows for direct access to the Federal Reserve Economic Data (FRED) website (http://research.stlouisfed .org) from within Excel, without using a browser. Once the basic functionality of the FRED add-in is mastered, the student can access variables from many different sources without having to learn each site's interface.

FRED's coverage is impressive. The add-in accesses a continually growing list of variables (several hundred thousand as of this writing) in the FRED database, including all major macroeconomic variables on output, prices, employment, interest, and money for a variety of countries. Once your students learn how to use this add-in, a whole world of information is made available from within Excel.

Using FRED is also advantageous for instructors. Updating data for a lecture or handout, long the bane of a harried professor rushing off to class, requires a single click. In addition, there is no need to constantly review instructions and test last semester's URLs to make sure they still work.

While FRED contains data from a wide variety of sources, it does not carry every single variable in the source. For example, only headline items from the National Income and Product Accounts (NIPA) are available at the time of this writing. It is possible, however, and demonstrated in the section on inflation, to merge data from an outside source into a spreadsheet with data downloaded from FRED.

This chapter shows how the FRED add-in can be used to access commonly used macro variables from several different sites. For each variable, the first screencast is the easiest, with basic downloads and analyses, and then more advanced work follows. While definitions and concepts are mentioned in the screencasts, it is expected that some kind of background source (e.g., a lecture, book, or handout) is being used to provide basic information.

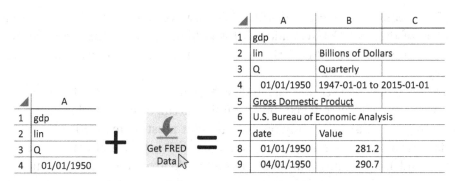

Figure 4.1.1. How the FRED add-in works.

The screencasts were done a few years ago and will remain for posterity (unless terribly wrong or Excel changes so radically that they become unintelligible). This time lag provides an advantage in that, as the years unfold, there is a natural sense of wonder and discovery in comparing the state of the world in the screencast to the current situation. Even for simple replications, for example, tracking inflation or unemployment over time, students will view a screencast with data up to 2012 or 2013 but be able to see what has happened the last few years. For some variables, presumably, something exciting and different may have occurred in the recent past or be unfolding in a current crisis situation.

The actual installation of the add-in is done once and should take no more than a few minutes. A five-minute introductory video is available at http:// research.stlouisfed.org/fred-addin. After the FRED add-in is installed, the **Quick Start** button in the **FRED** tab offers a brief summary of commands. The complete user's guide (for Windows computers) is available at http:// research.stlouisfed.org/fred-addin/FRED_PC_Users_Guide.pdf.

In essence, as Figure 4.1.1 shows, the user inputs the Series ID of a variable in the first row of a blank worksheet; the data manipulation, if any, in the next row (lin is the default); the frequency aggregation, if any, in the third row; and an optional start date in the next row. Clicking the **Get FRED Data** button downloads the data into the sheet and adds a link in the fifth row which launches a browser and takes you to the FRED website, where much more detail and documentation are available. The only required input is the Series ID in the first row. The screencasts explore a variety of ways to get data.

For a quick introduction to the FRED add-in, visit http://www.depauw .edu/learn/macroexcel/exceladdins/index.htm#FRED. Housing starts are used as an example to show how the FRED add-in works. This link can be sent to students unfamiliar with the add-in, and they should be up and running fairly quickly.

The screencasts are created with a Windows computer, but there is a Mac version of the FRED Excel add-in. It is not as smooth as the Windows version, but it works, and it is fairly easy to replicate the screencasts using Mac Excel.

The variables and screencasts in this chapter merely scratch the surface of the ways in which current economic conditions can be conveyed using FRED data. Instead of a static body of material that must be memorized, a better pedagogical strategy is to provide students with a tool that can be used to access and analyze information about the world around us. Developing data acquisition and critical thinking skills is vastly superior to the traditional textbook approach with dated tables and graphs.

One example of how FRED can be harnessed comes from McCracken and Ng (2015), who have created a big-data, macroeconomic database. FRED-MD offers three improvements over its rivals: (1) it will be updated monthly (MD stands for "monthly database," and there is a quarterly version also); (2) it uses public, free data from FRED; and (3) all data changes and revisions are incorporated into each update. Anyone who has ever regularly maintained data knows that this last point is a real time saver. The 134-variable FRED-MD and FRED-QD databases are available at http://research.stlouisfed.org/econ/mccracken/fred-databases.

Once the basic operation of the FRED add-in is mastered, downloading and analyzing data becomes routine. FRED's **Frequency Aggregation** button enables quick conversion to and from daily, monthly, quarterly, and annual data; and the data manipulation button makes it easy to compute percentage change year on year or at a compound annualized rate. Tasks that were incredibly time consuming and error prone are made trivial. This may sound impossible, but students will use the FRED add-in to explore variables and answer questions on their own – without supervision or to fulfill a course assignment. It absolutely invites search and inquiry. This alone is sufficient to include the FRED add-in throughout the economics curriculum.

Make sure to tell your students that there is even a FRED app for phones and tablets. Visit http://research.stlouisfed.org/fred-mobile to download and install it. Perhaps one day students will be poking their phones in class and it will not be because they are playing or on social media but because they are getting the latest GDP or inflation numbers from the FRED app.

Sources and Further Reading

The epigraph is from R. Solow, "Teaching Economics in the 1980s," *Journal of Economic Education* 14, no. 2 (1983): 65, http://www.jstor.org/stable/1182796. Solow's stress on the importance and difficulty of teaching economics, especially macroeconomics, applies today as well as it did in 1983. There is no reason to believe this will change in the foreseeable future.

A video series of short tutorials for using the FRED Excel add-in is available at http://fredqa.stlouisfed.org/2013/06/07/fred-video-series-from-nyu-stern.

"Okun's Law and FRED," at http://fredqa.stlouisfed.org/2012/03/28/okuns-law-and-fred, shows how to download data from FRED to estimate Okun's famous relationship between unemployment and real GDP.

Help with FRED is here: http://research.stlouisfed.org/fred2/help-faq. E-mail stlsFRED@stls.frb.org for support. They respond quickly (usually in a few hours and at most within one business day).

McCracken, W., and S. Ng. 2015. "FRED-MD: A Monthly Database for Macroeconomic Research." Working Paper 2015-012A. http://research.stlouisfed.org/wp/2015/2015-012.pdf.

4.2

GDP: *GDP.xls*

> The NIPAs trace their origin back to the 1930s, when the
> lack of comprehensive economic data hampered efforts to
> develop policies to combat the Great Depression. In
> response to this need, the U.S. Department of Commerce
> commissioned future Nobel Laureate Simon Kuznets to
> develop estimates of national income.
> – BEA Documentation

Quick Summary

To access *GDP.xls*, visit

http://www.depauw.edu/learn/macroexcel/excelworkbooks/Data/GDP.xls.

GDP.xls explains how to use the FRED Excel add-in to access GDP data
and offers several simple analyses using GDP. The focus is on understanding
basic national income accounting and becoming aware of a few facts about
GDP, including the current state of the economy. Investment is highlighted
as the most volatile of the major aggregate expenditure categories, and it is
decomposed in two ways: (1) as replacement and net investment and (2) into
its three main components, fixed nonresidential, residential, and changes in
business inventories.

Screencasts

- http://vimeo.com/econexcel/gdpshares: download U.S. GDP data and show that
  $GDP = C + I + G + NX$; also computes shares of GDP for $C, I,$ and G, showing
  that C is the largest of the three
- http://vimeo.com/econexcel/gdpfluctuations: download real and potential GDP
  and the FRED add-in's graphing tool plots the two series; percentage change data
  are used to better illustrate fluctuations and the fact that I is volatile and primarily
  responsible for variability in GDP

- http://vimeo.com/econexcel/gdpinvcomponents: download three components of investment: (1) tools, plant, and equipment; (2) housing; and (3) changes in business inventories in an attempt to find the source of volatility in investment; in addition to simply plotting the three over time, they are converted into standard units.

Introduction

Every macro book has definitions of various categories of aggregate spending, along with graphics of circular flows and descriptions of the system of national accounts used to produce familiar statistics on income and output. None of this is repeated here. Instead, the focus is on obtaining GDP and its components from FRED and gaining familiarity with the current state of the economy.

The *GDP.xls* workbook presents only the most fundamental concepts. FRED has an absolute treasure trove of national income aggregates. It makes sense to search FRED's database and develop your own exercises and examples. In fact, FRED is so easy to use that you can safely assign open-ended discovery and exploration tasks for your students. They can and will find interesting variables and relationships.

Common Problems for Students

The biggest hurdle for students is inadequate understanding of fundamental concepts. It is tempting to get bogged down in the minutiae of national income accounting to get definitions exactly right, but the opportunity cost of this approach can be quite high because there is so much other important information to cover. Taking inventory of core concepts before deciding what to include will help emphasize what is truly important. Here is my short list, a version of which is included in the *GDP.xls* workbook:

- Gross domestic product (GDP) is the market value of all final goods and services produced within a country in a given period of time.
- GDP is a flow, not a stock – it measures output per time period, not a total accumulated at a point in time. This crucial idea (along with a rejection of bullion as the source of the wealth of nations) was the basis of Adam Smith's attack on mercantilists of his day and forms the basis of his famous opening sentence in *The Wealth of Nations*:

The annual* labour of every nation is the fund which originally supplies it with all the necessaries and conveniencies of life which it annually consumes, and which consist always either in the immediate produce of that labour, or in what is purchased with that produce from other nations. (Smith [1776] 1904)

*[This word, with "annually" just below, at once marks the transition from the older British economists' ordinary practice of regarding the wealth of a nation as an

accumulated fund. Following the physiocrats, Smith sees that the important thing is how much can be produced in a given time.] {Note that this is Edwin Cannan's explanatory note and not included in Smith's original work.}

- GDP = $C + I + G + NX$. This fundamental equation expresses the fact that GDP can be computed as the sum of consumption (C), investment (I), government spending (G), and net exports (NX).
- There are two other ways to compute GDP: (1) the income approach, that is, sum the payments received by every factor of production, and (2) the product approach, that is, count every final good and service produced, multiply by its price, and sum. The product approach is usually implemented as a value-added computation at each stage of the production process.
- The three ways are equivalent in theory, but there are statistical discrepancies in practice. See Landefeld et al. (2008) for details.
- A circular flow diagram shows that GDP can be interpreted as both output and income; these are two sides of the same coin. This concept will play an important role in income-expenditure models.
- C, I, and G are expenditures (purchased final goods and services) made by consumers, firms, and governments, respectively. A computer purchase can be C, I, or G, depending on who bought it.
- It is easy to forget that G does not include transfer payments (such as Social Security benefits). *Government spending* in the macroeconomic sense means the purchase of final goods and services by governments, for example, roads, schools, and military gear.
- It is even harder to remember and really understand that investment does not represent investing in stocks or other speculative activity.
- While the core meaning of I is the purchase of new tools, plant, and equipment by firms, it also includes residential investment (new housing construction) and changes in business inventories.
- Inventories (produced but unsold output) are a critical part of I. Pointing out that inventories can be interpreted as self-purchasing goes a long way toward explaining how changes in inventories are included in I.
- Expenditures on some goods and services have to be imputed because they are not directly observed. For example, the rental value of owner-occupied housing has to be estimated (if not, GDP would fall if a renter bought the house).
- Sales of existing homes (or cars or anything used) are not expenditures on goods produced during the given time period, so they are not counted as part of GDP.
- Computing GDP in practice is unbelievably complicated. There are many weaknesses and missing data, so much so that the actual number for GDP is not especially important. The focus is on the percentage change in real GDP, based on the argument that the mismeasurement remains relatively constant over time. The *Intro* sheet has a stylized graph to support this argument.
- There are many ways in which GDP is flawed, but it remains the most fundamental measure of economic performance.

Perhaps this list will serve as a useful starting point in creating your own GDP highlights. There are undoubtedly many more ways (especially once we move to international accounting and balance of payments) that students fail to grasp the meaning behind the letters representing macro aggregates. Mentioning these while working with the data is a good strategy. This gives the student another way to connect the dots and remember basic information about GDP and its components.

Another potential stumbling block for undergraduate students involves presenting a litany of criticisms of GDP and national income accounts. While we can all agree that GDP does not measure happiness or social welfare, suffers from a variety of theoretical and practical deficiencies, and says nothing about the distribution of output, stressing these concerns at the beginning can be counterproductive for someone trying to understand how output and productivity are measured. Best practice teaching requires a gradual pace, with content delivered in calculated doses. Leave the list of inadequacies of GDP for the end, after the student has learned that GDP is how we measure economic performance and growth.

2013 NIPA Revisions

On July 31, 2013, the BEA rolled out a major, comprehensive revision of NIPA data back to 1929. Attempts to improve measurement of business investment by including research and development of intellectual property such as software and movies received widespread media attention. In addition, the base year for chained, real GDP was updated to 2009.

The screencasts and hidden sheets in the *GDP.xls* workbook are based on data before the revision date. Real GDP, for example, is in units of billions of chained 2005 dollars in the screencast but has since been updated. While a perfect replication of the numbers in the screencasts and hidden sheets is no longer possible through FRED, the fundamental ideas (such as the volatility of investment) remain unchanged. One side benefit of this major revision is easy detection of cheating by using the hidden sheets in the workbook – since real GDP is no longer measured in billions of chained 2005 dollars, a student answer using chained 2005 dollars is a definite red flag that should be investigated.

If old data are needed, consider these two options. ALFRED, the archival economic database at http://alfred.stlouisfed.org, maintains vintage data available at specific dates in history. A more general solution (useful for any website) is the Wayback Machine at the Internet Archive project, http://archive.org/web/web.php, which constantly crawls the Web and stores it. Simply enter the desired website (e.g., bea.gov) and a calendar is displayed with dates when the site was saved. Click on a date to see the website at that time.

Brief Screencast Descriptions

1. Components and Shares of GDP: The first screencast goes slowly and uses the FRED add-in's search tool to find data on GDP and its categories. It shows how GDP is composed of expenditures by consumers, firms, and governments, with an adjustment for net exports. Selecting "Gross Domestic Product" under "Browse Popular Data Releases" reveals the structure of the system of national accounts. Shares of GDP are computed revealing that consumption is by far the largest share, about two-thirds of GDP, while *I* and *G* are much smaller, with *NX* making up the small remainder.

   The screencast shows how to get more information on a variable by clicking its hyperlink in the fifth row of the spreadsheet. This provides access to the variable in the FRED website, and it can then be traced further to its source, for example, bea.gov in the case of GDP aggregates.

   Given that this is an introduction to using FRED, the first task associated with the screencast simply asks for a replication of the screencast, using the most up-to-date figures. There is a hidden sheet in the workbook, *GDPScreencast1*, which contains the data downloaded and analyzed in the screencast.

   The screencast mentions that we are interested in real, not nominal, GDP but does not compare them. To highlight that the GDP deflator is an important by-product of nominal and real GDP, assign the second task, which illustrates the relationship between these two measures. The student downloads quarterly real GDP (*GDPC96*), nominal GDP (*GDP*), and the GDP deflator (*GDPDEF*). The data are used to verify that *GDPC96 = GDP/GDPDEF*. A chart of real and nominal GDP over time shows that the latter grows much faster because it includes rising prices.

   For an interesting comparison, search FRED to obtain the breakdown of Chinese GDP. There are a variety of options (including Penn World Tables data on PPP adjusted shares of per capita GDP), but no matter what is used, the remarkably low share of consumer demand in gross domestic product is easily spotted.

2. Fluctuations in GDP and the Volatility of Investment: This screencast explains the phenomenon of economic fluctuations by charting real GDP and real potential GDP (*POTGDP*). Over a long time period, the changes in GDP are difficult to see. Displaying the percentage change over time clearly shows the variability in real GDP. Which of the three aggregate expenditures is driving the ups and downs in GDP? Plotting the percentage change of *C*, *I*, and *G* (including being careful to make the axes the same) reveals that *I* is markedly more volatile than *C* and *G*. Reveal the hidden *GDPScreencast2* sheet to see the data and analysis produced during the screencast. Finally, this screencast shows how to use the add-in's **Build Graph** to make a chart. Note that the chart format is line, instead of the usual scatter type.

   The task has the student replicate the analysis for another country, focusing especially on the volatility of investment. The **Browse Popular International Data** button in the ribbon lists eight countries, but other countries can be found by using the search tool. In a class setting, each student can be assigned a country and asked to present the results. To compare volatility across countries, a table of averages

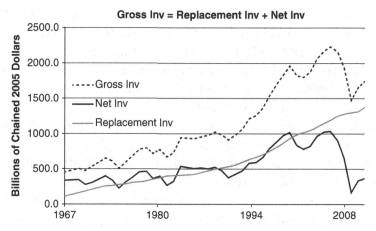

Figure 4.2.1. Net investment as the source of volatility in gross investment. *Source:* Hidden *GDPT4* sheet in *GDP.xls*.

and standard deviations of the percentage changes in GDP, *C*, *I*, and *G* would be a good group assignment or independent study project.

3. Components of Investment: The final screencast breaks down real gross domestic investment into tools, plant, and equipment purchased by firms (real private nonresidential fixed investment, *PNFIC1*), housing (real private residential fixed investment, *PRFIC1*), and changes in business inventories (*CBI*). The hope is to identify volatility in one of the components as the driving force in the volatility of gross investment, but this does not happen. All three subcategories seem to contribute in differing ways.

Given the different magnitudes of the series, the screencast shows how to standardize each variable and then plots each of the components with gross investment. This produces a different view of the complicated relationships but still does not reveal a monocausal explanation of the volatility of *I*. Reveal the hidden *GDP-Screencast3* sheet to see the data and analysis produced during the screencast.

This screencast uses the FRED add-in's **Build Graph** to make a chart and then extends it by adding a fourth series by copying and pasting the SERIES formula. This makes clear that the add-in is creating an Excel chart that can be manipulated by the usual methods.

The task breaks down gross investment along different lines, into replacement and net investment. The student is asked to create a chart like Figure 4.2.1 and identify a source for the volatility of *I*. Unlike the screencast, it is clear that net investment is driving the volatility of gross investment. Replacement investment seems to rise somewhat steadily over time (as the economy grows), but pronounced swings in net investment match the variation in *I*.

Conclusion

The FRED Excel add-in provides a complement to the standard exposition of tables and definitions in the textbook and lecture. This section focused on three fundamental concepts that are sure to be covered: (1) GDP can be measured as the sum of expenditures by consumers, firms, and governments (plus *NX*, of course); (2) GDP fluctuates, with investment being especially volatile; and (3) macro aggregates such as investment comprise subcategories that can be examined. Unfortunately, there does not appear to be a single source for the volatility of investment.

Although the emphasis of this section is on data, the *LRvSR* sheet does present a brief overview of macroeconomics, highlighting short- versus long-run perspectives. A stylized graph of trend and actual GDP (see Figure 2.2.2) is used in the *LRvSR* sheet to convey how GDP can be studied in terms of its cyclical or trend behavior. *Money.xls* (Section 4.5) has an HP filter function and a task asks the student to separate trend from cycle in GDP. It is important to make sure that students understand the separation between long and short run in macroeconomics. In addition to changing focus from growth to business cycle, the analysis of shocks depends on the time horizon.

Further data exploration with the FRED Excel add-in can go in many directions. For example, search in FRED for "PPP" to get Penn World Tables (http://cid.econ.ucdavis.edu/pwt.html) purchasing power parity adjusted data and make international comparisons in living standards. There is a wealth of federal budget data if deficit and debt to GDP ratios over time are desired. Drilling down into subcategories such as new home construction, motor vehicle production, energy, and health aggregates (via the **Browse Popular US Aggregates** button or searching) is also an instructive way to develop awareness of current economic conditions.

Sources and Further Reading

The epigraph is from "Concepts and Methods of the U.S. National Income and Product Accounts," November 2012, 1–2, http://www.bea.gov/methodologies/index.htm, and answers the question, How did the NIPAs originate? It is noteworthy that the person instrumental in setting up British national income accounts, Richard Stone, also received a Nobel Prize in Economic Sciences. Establishing a coherent, reliable methodology for aggregate measures of economic performance is not trivial.

There are many sources that explain categories and computation of GDP, but an especially clear exposition can be found in J. Landefeld, E. Seskin, and B. Fraumeni, "Taking the Pulse of the Economy: Measuring GDP," *Journal of Economic Perspectives* 22, no. 2 (2008): 193–216.

Smith, A. (1776) 1904. *An Inquiry into the Nature and Causes of the Wealth of Nations.* Methuen. http://www.econlib.org/library/Smith/smWN.html.

4.3

Unemployment: *Unem.xls*

> The outstanding faults of the economic society in which
> we live are its failure to provide for full employment and
> its arbitrary and inequitable distribution of wealth
> and incomes.
> – John Maynard Keynes

Quick Summary

To access *Unem.xls*, visit

http://www.depauw.edu/learn/macroexcel/excelworkbooks/Data/Unem.xls.

Unem.xls explains how to use the FRED Excel add-in to access labor market data. The focus is on understanding basic concepts (such as the unemployment rate and the labor force participation rate) and becoming aware of a few labor market facts, including the current state of the economy. Additional topics include seasonal adjustment, sampling, and a simple job search model.

Screencasts

- http://vimeo.com/econexcel/unemintro: download data on the unemployment rate and plot it (with recession bars); other variables are downloaded and basic definitions are illustrated with the data
- http://vimeo.com/econexcel/unemgroups: download unemployment data on various subgroups and illustrate that the impact of unemployment on particular categories of people is extremely variable
- http://vimeo.com/econexcel/unemseasonaladj: Excel's **PivotTable** tool is used to find the monthly average in seasonally adjusted and not seasonally adjusted unemployment rates to show the seasonal pattern in the data
- http://vimeo.com/econexcel/unemlfpr: download data on the labor force participation rate and show the striking difference in men's and women's LFPR since World War II

- http://vimeo.com/econexcel/unemsampling: explains the idea of sampling variability by sampling from a hypothetical population in Excel and using simulation to show the results from many samples
- http://vimeo.com/econexcel/unemsearch: implements and solves a fixed sample search model with Monte Carlo simulation

Introduction

FRED provides access to data from the Current Population Survey (CPS), which is the source of labor market measures such as unemployment and labor force participation rates. It also includes international measures of unemployment rates, harmonized for equivalent definitions of job search, from the Organisation for Economic Co-operation and Development (OECD). Although not covered here, FRED also serves up data from Current Employment Statistics (CES, which is also known as the establishment survey) and the Job Openings and Labor Turnover Survey (JOLTS). Thus, the FRED Excel add-in offers easily available, timely information on a wide variety of labor market indicators.

Definitions of variables and details on household surveys are left to textbooks and lecture notes. The *Intro* sheet contains a minimal review, including a layout of the framework used to organize various states of labor market activity and a few basic definitions. This should not replace, however, a more comprehensive presentation of labor market surveys and how they work.

Although the focus is on downloading data, the screencasts show how to create charts with the FRED add-in's graphing tools and Excel's own scatterplot. For the latter, the default origin of zero forces explanation of dates in Excel and how to adjust the *x* axis. More sophisticated analysis is adopted for seasonal adjustment where Excel's **PivotTable** tool is used to find monthly averages.

The *Unem.xls* workbook includes two sheets (accessible from a button in the *ToDo* sheet) that are much more advanced than the usual fare. The *Sampling* sheet sets up a mock survey and enables random sampling from a population. Simulation is used to make clear the variability in sample outcomes. The *JobSearch* sheet also uses simulation to present a job search model. It can be used to show that frictional unemployment will rise if search costs fall. Both of these applications are far from the mainstream curriculum, but they demonstrate the powerful pedagogy of concrete, visual exposition.

Common Problems for Students

Unlike national income accounts, with terms like *investment* that have popular meaning different from the technical definition, labor market statistics are reasonably clear. Most students grasp the key idea behind the definition of unemployment – jobless but seeking work, as opposed to being out of the labor force – but they seem to forget that the denominator in the unemployment rate is the labor force. In fact, conceptual difficulties with ratios, in general, may be the source of confusion with many labor market measures, which rely heavily on proportions.

One obvious teaching strategy is to always present a rate with its numerator and denominator clearly displayed. Repetition is a good way to develop familiarity and understanding. The *Intro* sheet's visual display of various categories provides an overall view that may help some students grasp the logic underlying the unemployment rate and other labor statistics.

Tasks and Answers

The resulting spreadsheet at the end of each screencast and accompanying answers for tasks are saved inside *Unem.xls*. These sheets are not merely hidden and cannot be accessed by unhiding them. They can be revealed by running the *ToggleHideUnhide* macro (with keyboard shortcut CTRL-SHIFT-U). They are organized in sequential order, with each screencast followed by its task answer. Run the *ToggleHideUnhide* macro again to conceal the sheets.

Note that the screencasts and answers were produced some time ago. Student answers (or your own replications) will and should have data up to the moment. Perfect reproduction of an answer key may indicate cheating of some kind.

Brief Screencast Descriptions

1. Introduction to the Unemployment Rate: The first screencast downloads the unemployment rate at an annual frequency since 1948 and uses FRED's graphing tool to make a chart with recession bars. The voice-over emphasizes the variability in the unemployment rate and its association with recessions. Next, data on civilian working-age population, labor force, out of the labor force, and unemployed are downloaded. Adding those in and out of the labor force equals the civilian population aged sixteen years and older, and dividing the number of employed by the labor force yields the unemployment rate. This reinforces definitions of these labor market statistics.

   This screencast has two tasks: (1) compare the harmonized unemployment rate of two other countries to the United States and (2) compare the unemployment rate and employment ratio (number employed divided by working-age population). Both tasks offer engaging work, and the first one can be used in a group setting, with each student reporting on several countries. Note that searching for "harmonized unemployment rate" provides data on many more countries that those listed in the **Browse Popular International Data** button. Also, broader measures of unemployment (such as the increasingly popular *U6*, with FRED ID U6RATE) are available.

2. The Unemployment Rate by Group: This screencast is devoted to the lesson that unemployment hits different groups wildly unevenly. Unemployment rates for men aged 20 years and older, women aged 20 years and older, and 16- to 19-year-olds are downloaded. A graph shows that teenagers have a much higher unemployment rate than older men and women. A comparison of men and women reveals that the Great Recession produced much higher unemployment rates for men than women. The screencast shows how to work with dates in Excel and change the minimum *x* axis value to the date of the first observation.

   The task has students download unemployment rate by educational attainment. They will produce a chart that makes clear that unemployment rates are lower for more educated groups. This chart is in the *T2* sheet, which is visible after running the *ToggleHideUnhide* macro (with keyboard shortcut CTRL-SHIFT-U). This task also includes a Show Me button that reveals a comparison of unemployment rates for men and women without high school degrees. These data were not available within FRED and were downloaded from the BLS website.

   Of course, the unemployment rate can be viewed from the perspective of many other groups. Click the FRED add-in's **Browse Popular Data Releases** and select **Household Survey** to get unemployment rates by race and ethnicity. Use the search tool to get unemployment rates for specific geographic regions such as states or major metropolitan areas.

3. Seasonal Adjustment: This screencast uses Excel's **PivotTable** feature to explain seasonal adjustment. Adjusted and raw unemployment monthly rates since 1948 are downloaded and Excel's TEXT function is used to create two new columns, MONTH and YEAR. A PivotTable of average unemployment rate by month is created, and it shows the pattern in the unadjusted series and how it has been removed from the seasonally adjusted data.

   The task has the student replicate the procedure for U6, a much broader measure of unemployment that includes discouraged and marginally attached workers. Running the *ToggleHideUnhide* macro (with keyboard shortcut CTRL-SHIFT-U) reveals the *PivotTables* sheets along with the screencast and task sheets.

4. The Labor Force Participation Rate: This short screencast shows the amazing changes in the labor force participation rate (LFPR) for men and women in the United States since World War II. While men's LFPR steadily fell, women's rapidly rose after the mid-1960s. The overall LFPR masks these two opposing trends.

   The task has students compare LFPR for Japan, Italy, and the United States. The assignment is more challenging because specific Series IDs are not provided. Exploration of LFPR in other countries is enlightening and interesting and, therefore, ideal for group presentations or independent study projects.

5. Sampling Variability: This topic is ambitious, but simulation makes it accessible to good students. The basic point is not difficult to understand: since the

unemployment rate is based on a sample survey, it is a random variable with a sampling distribution. The standard error (SE) for the overall, official unemployment rate (U3) is about 0.1 of a percentage point. Sampling variability is shown via Monte Carlo simulation of sampling from a fixed population.

Clicking the MC Sim button is powerful yet user-friendly. Any cell that changes when the sheet is recalculated is a candidate for analysis via simulation. In this example, we track the sample unemployment rate and the results are displayed in a new sheet. Comparative statics properties can be explored by changing a parameter and comparing simulation results.

The task is straightforward: replicate the screencast using LFPR instead of the unemployment rate. As expected, when the sample size increases, the SE falls. It is easy to verify that a student did his or her own work because the simulation results will be different for every student.

To access the *Sampling* sheet, click the Show Sampling button in the *ToDo* sheet. Although it is explained in the screencast and clearly stated on the spreadsheet, the DRAWSAMPLE function is an array function and the keyboard combination CTRL-SHIFT-ENTER is required. Hit the ESC (escape) key to return to the spreadsheet.

The *Sampling* sheet has a variety of cell formulas for the superpopulation that are not explained in the screencast. Excel's RAND() function, which is uniformly distributed on $[0, 1)$, is used in a variety of ways to draw gender, age, and whether the person works (if 16 or older) or is in the labor force (if not working). Neither the employment nor unemployment probability depends on age in this hypothetical data generation process.

6. Job Search: This final screencast is rather advanced and not part of the conventional intermediate macroeconomics curriculum, but Excel's ability to simulate chance processes makes it an attractive topic. A fixed sample search model is implemented and solved via simulation. Lowering the cost of search leads to an increase in the number of jobs sampled and a higher unemployment rate.

The screencast focuses solely on simulation, but the mathematical solution is also presented starting in row 100. The reduced-form expression makes clear that the optimal number of jobs sampled is an increasing function of the highest paying job and a decreasing function of the cost of search. This optimization problem is rather simple, so this is not an example of a situation where simulation provides an approximate answer when no closed-form, analytical solution is available. If your students can handle the calculus, show the analytical result and emphasize how the two methods yield the same answers; if not, use only simulation (like the screencast does).

This topic has two tasks. The first is easier. It has the student finish the argument made in the screencast that the optimal number of jobs to sample increases from three to four when the cost of search falls from 0.0625 to 0.04.

The second task is essentially a comparative statics analysis of the maximum pay parameter. The student is asked to explore the effect of increasing maximum pay from 1 to 1.5625. This parameter value was chosen so that the optimal number of offers increases from three to four. The student should be able to use simulation to determine that sampling four jobs is the optimal solution. As noted in the description of the previous screencast, simulation results will be different for every student. Identical results are highly likely to involve cheating of some kind.

Conclusion

Unem.xls uses the FRED add-in to download labor market data for the United States from the CPS and internationally harmonized unemployment and labor force participation rates. The workbook assumes a basic understanding of concepts and uses data to reinforce definitions. The primary goal is awareness of historical trends and current labor market conditions.

Excel highlights in the topics covered in this section include using PivotTables to explain seasonal adjustment and use of simulation to illustrate sampling variability and solve a job search model. Both PivotTables and simulation have much wider applicability, but they may require additional teaching resources and time. These are advanced topics for undergraduates that can be easily integrated into other courses (such as courses on labor economics).

As mentioned in the introduction, FRED provides access to JOLTS and CES data. Use JOLTS to explore job openings, hires, and separations, while wages and employment from the firm's point of view are available through the CES. Duration of unemployment is an important topic that was not covered in the screencasts but can be easily accessed through FRED. Finally, the family of variables on productivity and costs (click the **Browse Popular Data Releases** button) is another resource for expanding your students' familiarity with current economic conditions and measures of economic performance.

Sources and Further Reading

The epigraph is from the opening sentence of the last chapter of J. M. Keynes, *The General Theory of Employment, Interest and Money* (1936), http://www.marxists .org/reference/subject/economics/keynes/general-theory.

An overview of seasonal adjustment is in a BLS technical bulletin, "Seasonal Adjustment" (February 2004). Employment and earnings are available online at http://www.bls.gov/cps/eetech_seas.pdf. The BLS maintains a list of resources on seasonal adjustment here: http://www.bls.gov/cps/documentation.htm.

Simulation in Excel is the foundation of H. Barreto and F. Howland, *Introductory Econometrics with Microsoft Excel Using Monte Carlo Simulation* (Cambridge University Press, 2008), http://www.wabash.edu/econometrics. Implementing chance processes in Excel, repeating the process many times, and directly observing the results is a powerful way to teach and learn.

4.4

Inflation: *Inflation.xls*

> After a long period in which the desired direction for inflation was always downward, we are now [2003] in a situation in which risks to the inflation rate can be either upward, toward excessive inflation, or downward, toward too-low inflation or deflation.
> – Ben Bernanke

Quick Summary

To access *Inflation.xls*, visit

http://www.depauw.edu/learn/macroexcel/excelworkbooks/Data/Inflation.xls.

Inflation.xls explains how to use the FRED Excel add-in to review the historical record of inflation in the United States and to gain familiarity with inflation rate performance across countries. There is emphasis on computation in calculating the inflation rate as the percentage change in the price index and in using the price index to deflate nominal series. Four indexes, CPI, GDP deflator, the Fed's core inflation (PCE less food and energy), and chained CPI are examined.

Screencasts

- http://vimeo.com/econexcel/inflationusahistory: examines the historical record of price variability since World War II, as measured by the CPI, in the United States; the last episode of severe inflation occurred in the 1970s, and since then, the United States has enjoyed relative price stability
- http://vimeo.com/econexcel/inflationcollegetuition: downloads data from the BLS on the college tuition price index and compares it to the overall CPI; the results are dramatic – college tuition has risen twice as fast as overall prices – and it also makes clear that data from other sources can be merged in a spreadsheet with FRED downloads, which is a simple but powerful point

- http://vimeo.com/econexcel/inflationrealvalues: shows how to deflate a nominal series of postage stamp prices with a price index to create a series of real postage stamp prices in 2012 dollars; task uses data for minimum wage; long CPI series back to 1790
- http://vimeo.com/econexcel/inflationcomparing: downloads the CPI, GDP deflator, core inflation, and chained CPI; compares them and explains why we have competing price indexes

Introduction

As with GDP and unemployment, this section assumes a book or other background reading is providing definitions and explanations of price index theory. The *Intro* sheet provides a brief review via a listing of important concepts (which might form the basis of a lecture on inflation), and the *CPI* sheet describes the weights for the eight major categories in the CPI-U market basket, but the focus of the screencasts is primarily on practical computations and empirical data.

No mention is made of seasonal adjustment, which is covered in the previous section on unemployment. The effect of inflation on nominal interest rates is also absent, deferred until the Fisher Effect is presented in the next section. Finally, causal explanations of inflation are not discussed. The goal is simply to observe inflation patterns and learn how to use a price index to deflate a nominal variable.

Common Problems for Students

With respect to the inflation rate, it is understandable that the bewildering array of options for measuring inflation is terribly confusing to students. How can there be so many different inflation rates, sometimes wildly different from each other? As usual, the best approach is to tackle this head-on with a clear, organized presentation that directly answers this question.

Any introduction of inflation should begin by separating the theoretical abstraction of the price level from how the price level is measured via a price index. Yes, inflation is a process of continuously rising prices, and we always compute an inflation rate the same way as the percentage change in the price index, but there are many different price indexes to choose from. By stressing the fact that the price level is a theoretical ideal that runs into immediate problems when it is operationalized, the student has a way to understand why various measures of inflation exist.

The explanation of the presence of multiple measures of inflation is strengthened by pointing out the impossible nature of the task: to reduce a variety of individual price movements to a single number. This is known as the index number problem. Since there are many ways to construct a price index that compresses individual variation into an overall average and no unambiguously best approach, this explains why we can produce different inflation rates from the same data.

The standard presentation of inflation that begins by defining fixed-price and fixed-quantity indexes via formulas and providing hypothetical examples of price and quantity for two goods over a few years is tedious and ineffective. Instead of starting in the middle of a complicated story, mired in perplexing detail, consider framing the material around the question of why we have so many ways to measure inflation. Highlight that the computation itself, the percentage change in the price index, is always the same – we get different measures of inflation because we use different price indexes.

Tasks and Answers

The resulting spreadsheet at the end of each screencast and accompanying answers for tasks are saved inside *Inflation.xls*. These sheets are not merely hidden and cannot be accessed by unhiding them. They can be revealed by running the *ToggleHideUnhide* macro (with keyboard shortcut CTRL-SHIFT-U). They are organized in sequential order, with each screencast followed by its task answer. Run the *ToggleHideUnhide* macro again to conceal the sheets.

Brief Screencast Descriptions

1. Inflation Performance in the United States via the CPI: The first screencast downloads CPI-U all items (*Series ID CPIAUCSL*), which underlies the usual inflation rate reported by mainstream media. The voice-over stresses that inflation is the percentage change in the price index, not the price index itself, and uses the **pca** option to produce annualized percentage changes from monthly data. Unfortunately, monthly data obscure trend patterns, so the frequency is changed to annual and the historical record of high inflation in the 1970s and early 1980s followed by moderate price variability is made clear. Mention is made of deflation. The screencast concludes with an international comparison with France, which has a similar inflation record. The third screencast offers a much longer series, from 1790, of inflation in the United States with the annual CPI available in column B of sheet *3*.

   The associated task is to replicate the screencast with the latest available data and compare the inflation performance of another country to the United States. Results can be presented in a group setting, with each student reporting on a particular country. Of course, several countries could be assigned to each student or group. Note that using the FRED Excel add-in to search for "harmonized cpi" provides data on many more countries than those listed in the **Browse Popular International Data** button.

2. Inflation in a Specific Group: This screencast is devoted to the lesson that the overall inflation rate masks substantial variability in subgroups of goods and services. College tuition is chosen, but it is unavailable from within FRED. Fortunately, the bls.gov website is reasonably user-friendly, and it is used to download the desired data. The college tuition price index is copied and pasted next to the all items price index, and the two series are plotted. The result is stunning, with college tuition sporting double the monthly percentage of CPI-U – although the screencast does end with a warning that the sticker price may not be a good measure of actual prices paid and displays a chart of tuition, financial aid, and loans over time.

   The associated task is to compare prescription drug prices to the overall CPI. Run the *ToggleHideUnhide* macro (with keyboard shortcut CTRL-SHIFT-U) to reveal the answer sheet *T2*. If using bls.gov is deemed too difficult, substitute the group "Medical Care" or search FRED for a medical category. Again, assigning different specific items to each student or group and sharing results is informative and often energizes the classroom.

3. Using a Price Index to Create a Real Variable: This screencast shows how to create a real value by dividing a nominal value by a price index. Sheet *3* has annual CPI all the way back to 1790. Using data on postage stamps, first sold in 1885 for two cents, the stamp price series is deflated both in the original 1982–84 base year and in 2012 dollars (the data available when the screencast was created).

   The task repeats the procedure for the minimum wage. First instituted in 1938 at 25 cents per hour, the minimum wage was $7.25/hour in 2013. The student is asked to create a chart of nominal and real minimum wage and determine whether the current minimum wage is high by historical standards. Run the *ToggleHideUnhide* macro (with keyboard shortcut CTRL-SHIFT-U) to reveal the answer sheet *T3*. As of this writing, the quixotic, seemingly endless struggle to raise the minimum wage has gathered much steam (albeit on a piecemeal, state and city basis). Doing this task with the latest data if substantial changes in the federal minimum wage are enacted should make for an interesting, timely assignment for students.

   If calculating real prices is high priority, the annual CPI in sheet *3* can be used to deflate nominal prices of an almost endless array of examples. Average salary by sport captures interest, as do energy prices or concert tickets. Car, television, and computer prices would be useful for discussion of quality changes.

4. Comparing Price Indexes: This screencast compares CPI, GDP deflator, core inflation (PCE less food and energy), and chained CPI (C-CPI). Each of the other three is compared (in three separate charts) with the CPI with a general description of the index. The voice-over points out that the CPI is the most volatile and overshoots inflation by roughly a percentage point. The average annualized rates of inflation of the four indexes are compared and examples for when you would use each one are given. The screencast concludes with a reminder that measuring the price level, a theoretical abstraction, is not easy, and this explains why we have so many competing price indexes.

   The task utilizes the **Browse Popular International Data** button to have the student compare CPI all items to CPI less food and energy in a country other than the United States. Sharing results in class is an option.

Conclusion

Inflation.xls uses FRED to download CPI and other price indexes. Emphasis is placed on percentage change as a measure of inflation and using the price index to deflate nominal values. Definitions and formulas are left to background reading, although the links in the *Intro* sheet are excellent summaries of how the CPI works and its weaknesses.

A highlight of the material presented is a simple yet powerful idea: one can download data outside of FRED and merge it with FRED data. This is demonstrated in the second screencast on college tuition. Students need to be aware of FRED as a resource for empirical papers and projects, and although it seems like each day brings more variables into FRED, it does not take every piece of information from a source. But just because FRED cannot access every variable needed does not imply it should be abandoned. Use the convenience of FRED to get easily available variables, and then augment the spreadsheet with data from other sources.

The long series on CPI in sheet *3* (back to 1790) is a handy resource for creating real values for classroom lectures or handouts. In fact, this screencast alone could be used in other courses. Hiding or deleting other sheets in the workbook and renaming sheet *3* will not impair the workbook in any way.

As always, much is left unsaid. No mention is made of the fact that chained price indexes might be more accurate, but they do not have the additive properties that conventional, fixed-weight indexes provide. Perhaps even more frustrating is the focus on empirical data and the absence of theory. The next section on money tries to remedy this omission, although an explanation of the sources and root causes of inflation remains elusive.

Sources and Further Reading

The epigraph is from "An Unwelcome Fall in Inflation?," remarks by Governor Ben S. Bernanke before the Economics Roundtable, University of California, San Diego, La Jolla, California, July 23, 2003, http://www.federalreserve.gov/boarddocs/speeches/2003/20030723. In this talk, Bernanke explains the dangers associated with deflation and explains how the Fed would combat it, foreshadowing future policy.

The *Intro* sheet in *Inflation.xls* has links with recommended background sources on inflation.

4.5

Money: *Money.xls*

> Inflation is always and everywhere a monetary
> phenomenon in the sense that it is and can be produced
> only by a more rapid increase in the quantity of money
> than in output.
> – Milton Friedman

Quick Summary

To access *Money.xls*, visit

http://www.depauw.edu/learn/macroexcel/excelworkbooks/Data/Money.xls.

Money.xls explains how to use the FRED Excel add-in to examine a variety
of measures of the money supply and explore their relationship with inflation. *Money.xls* contains a Hodrick–Prescott (HP) filter function to separate
trend from cycle in macro aggregates. The workbook also has data from the
International Financial Statistics (IFS) on a subset of countries from which
seigniorage rates can be computed. The screencasts show how to download
and examine data on interest rates (including the Fisher effect) and exchange
rates.

Screencasts

- http://vimeo.com/econexcel/moneyinflation: downloads various monetary aggregates (M1, M2, and MZM) and tries (and fails) to show how inflation depends on
  the money supply (including a ten-year moving average)
- http://vimeo.com/econexcel/moneymsi: covers the rather advanced topic of
  Divisia monetary services indexes (MSI)
- http://vimeo.com/econexcel/moneyseigniorage: downloads data on base money
  and nominal GDP to compute seigniorage rates; has data from IFS for a small
  subset of countries
- http://vimeo.com/econexcel/moneyfftaylor: explains how the Taylor Rule versus
  the federal funds rate offers a window into how the Fed views the economy; evaluates the tenures of Fed chairs since 1970

- http://vimeo.com/econexcel/moneyfisher: downloads data on interest and inflation rates, showing that they move roughly together, and then explains the relationship via the Fisher Effect
- http://vimeo.com/econexcel/moneyxrates: downloads data on real effective exchange rates produced by the Fed and the OECD; looks at the trade share weights for the United States and comments on the relationship between money supply and exchange rates
- http://vimeo.com/econexcel/moneyhpfilter: shows how to use the HP array function in Excel to separate a variable into its trend and cyclical components using the Hodrick–Prescott algorithm

Introduction

As with GDP, unemployment, and inflation, the primary focus of this section is on awareness of historical trends and current economic conditions with respect to money, interest rates, and exchange rates. The task is complicated by the fact that the money supply is not easily measured, and a core theoretical result, that inflation depends on the rate of change of the money supply, is difficult to show with data.

As with other variables in this chapter, the workbook assumes a background reading or supplemental text of some sort. Nothing is said, for example, about the history and meaning of the quantity theory of money. A brief list of definitions and core ideas is included in the *Intro* sheet, but this is intended as a review.

Not surprisingly, the FRED database has a wealth of data on financial statistics, of which only a few are presented in the screencasts. Pull down the **Browse Popular Data Releases** menu item to reveal Federal Reserve balance sheet information, banking data, and much more.

The screencasts should be considered more in the nature of topics from which you can pick and choose than principles that must be covered. The HP filter function, in particular, is provided as a way to enable easy construction of charts for presentations and student papers, not as necessary material in an undergraduate macro course. Regardless of your favorite monetary aggregate or specific relationship between variables that you think your students must be made aware of, FRED is likely to have the data, and the FRED Excel add-in will be a convenient way to download and display those data.

Common Problems for Students

What could be simpler than money? Everybody needs and uses money, so surely we know what it is. This, of course, is the core of the problem for students because, in fact, money is a vague concept. By simply saying that money is not binary but actually a continuum, you may get an "Aha!" moment. At the very least, the many measures of money, starting from currency and including ever broader categories, will make a little more sense. Careful explanation of money as a sum of various types of financial assets will prove helpful when students are exposed to the familiar litany of monetary aggregates, M1, M2, and so on.

A second potential area of confusion, which should also be tackled head-on, is the notion of money demand. Money supply is relatively simple – the stock of money (however measured) at any point in time. Money demand is, at least superficially, trickier. Money demand requires understanding that there is an underlying optimization problem. The question is not "How much money do you want?" (to which the answer would seem to be "As much as I can get") but "How much of your wealth do you want to allocate to money versus your other assets?" A classic illustration is to point out that a million-aire (perhaps now it should be billionaire) may have a few thousand dollars in money holdings and the rest of the portfolio in stocks, bonds, and other nonmonetary assets.

Students are often completely unfamiliar with some terms, such as seignior-age, and building vocabulary requires effort, but money and money demand are especially confusing because they are so common. It takes repetition to really understand what these terms mean in a macroeconomics context. Blanchard and Johnson (2013, 65) offer a "Focus Box" on "Semantic Traps: Money, Income, and Wealth." They conclude with two directives:

Learn how to be economically correct:

Do not say "Mary is making a lot of money"; say "Mary has a high income."

Do not say "Joe has a lot of money"; say "Joe is very wealthy."

Semantic traps are everywhere in economics, and they really are traps for students and professors alike. Pointing this out will help your students master the jargon and learn economics.

Tasks and Answers

The resulting spreadsheet at the end of each screencast and accompanying answers for tasks are saved inside *Money.xls*. These sheets are not merely hid-den and cannot be accessed by unhiding them. They can be revealed by run-ning the *ToggleHideUnhide* macro (with keyboard shortcut CTRL-SHIFT-U). They are organized in sequential order, with each screencast followed by its task answer. Run the *ToggleHideUnhide* macro again to conceal the sheets.

Brief Screencast Descriptions

1. Monetary Aggregates and Inflation: This introductory screencast downloads and shows M1, M2, and money with zero maturity (MZM). The primary point is that

there are many measures of the money supply, and they behave differently. Innovation in financial instruments has created a challenging measurement problem. As a theoretical proposition, most economists (see Friedman's epigraph to this section) believe that money growth produces inflation, but it is not easy to see this in the data. The screencast shows M2 with annual inflation and then repeats the comparison with ten-year moving average rates of growth. Both fail to show a clear relationship between money growth and inflation. It concludes by showing two scatterplots from Mishkin (2011, 114): one has decade averages of money growth and inflation for the United States, and the other displays an international comparison of money growth and inflation. Both graphs support the claim that inflation is driven by money growth.

The task has the student construct a ten-year moving average comparison of inflation and MZM. This is no better at revealing a relationship between money growth and inflation than the M2 aggregate used in the screencast.

This screencast can be used as a jumping-off point for more sophisticated exploration of the relationship between money and inflation. One obvious point is that the connection is being confounded by other variables. By not holding anything else constant, we are getting a warped perspective. This path takes us to the quantity theory or other accounts of how money and inflation are connected.

Perhaps the explanation for the lack of a clear correlation between money growth and inflation lies in the measurement of money itself. Mishkin's view is quite clear: "The amount of information in the monetary aggregates is essentially zero" (Mandel 1999, 34). This leads to the next topic.

2. Measuring Money: This screencast is about the use of Divisia index numbers in measuring money. This topic is admittedly advanced, and the only textbook I have found that even mentions Divisia versions of monetary aggregates is Fisher (2001), but measurement of money really is an open scandal:

Is there any reason at all to prefer the disreputable simple-sum monetary aggregates to the state-of-the-art Divisia monetary aggregates? The answer to both questions is one simple unequivocal word – *no*! In measurement, central banks should do the best they can, not the worst they can. It doesn't get any worse than simple-sum aggregation. (Barnett 2011, Kindle location 1398–401)

The screencast keeps things uncomplicated by downloading Divisia M2 and comparing it to simple-sum M2. The explosive growth in simple-sum M2 in January 1983 is due to the arrival of money market funds. Other spikes (with dates revealed by conditional formatting), such as 9/11, are real. The remainder of the screencast is devoted to the monetarist experiment of 1979–82. Tracking simple-sum M2 (and other conventional aggregates) severely overstates the growth rate of money during that time. While inflation was brought under control, it seems the Fed was unaware of how restrictive monetary policy had become. Students will enjoy learning about this episode.

An Excel highlight of this screencast is its use of the *EconChart.xla* add-in (available at http://www.depauw.edu/learn/macroexcel/exceladdins) to zoom in on specific time intervals. The **Zoomer** control will work on any spreadsheet with scatter type charts. The only restriction is that panes must be unfrozen. Zooming is helpful while exploring data and for presentation.

The task involves replication of the 1979–82 episode with Divisia MZM (FRED *Series ID MSIMZMP*) instead of *MSIM2*. The results are stronger in that money growth during October 1979 to September 1982 was even lower with the MSI version of MZM than the simple-sum aggregate. Instead of money growth averaging 3.2% per year (as shown in the screencast using *MSIM2*), growth in Divisia MZM averaged only 1.2% per year.

Another assignment could be the replication of Table 1 in Barnett (1984), which offers a complete list of monthly growth rates at annualized rates during the monetarist experiment. The results with data from FRED come close but do not exactly coincide with the data Barnett used in 1984.

3. Seigniorage: This screencast shows how to use the list box with different countries in the *IFS* sheet to get data on nominal GDP and base money from the International Financial Statistics. Clicking on a country inserts a new sheet in the workbook with data for the selected country. The student then computes the change in base money and divides it by nominal GDP to get the seigniorage rate. The screencast does this for the United States and also computes the seigniorage rate using data from FRED. Not surprisingly, the two are very close.

The task is to select a country and report the seigniorage rate, along with an explanation of the extent to which the government used its power to issue money to finance its expenditures. Starting in cell CD100 of the *IFS* sheet, the average seigniorage rate for each country is computed to enable easy checking of student answers. If each student is assigned a country, the task can be made into an in-class presentation exercise.

The *IFS* sheet includes a brief description of seigniorage and a link to Fischer (1982). An additional assignment would be to compare a country's use of seigniorage in Fischer's data set and its performance since that time. A more ambitious project would entail updating Fischer's results for all of the countries in his sample.

4. The Federal Funds Rate and the Taylor Rule: This screencast downloads data on the federal funds rate and then explains the Taylor Rule. The emphasis is less on computation (the formulas are provided) and more on the logic of the Taylor Rule and how it responds to inflationary pressure and the GDP gap. The zero interest rate lower bound is obviously apparent when the federal funds rate is graphed and when the Taylor Rule yields a negative target interest rate.

The task is fairly straightforward and should be easily completed because the screencast covers the Burns and Bernanke tenures, and the answer depends on whether the fed funds rate is above or below its target rate. For the others, it is clear that Miller was more accommodating than the Taylor Rule suggests, while Volcker's monetary policy was more restrictive (which agrees with the second screencast on the monetarist experiment). Greenspan gets mixed reviews on this score – he began like Volcker but ended like Burns, with the federal funds rate substantially below the target during his last four years.

The inspiration for this screencast is from Cahill (2006), who has a step-by-step Excel lab version of the Taylor Rule. The *Taylor* sheet can be used in a lecture format to review the historical record of nominal interest rates in the United States for recent Fed chairs. It has excellent teaching potential going forward as more data come in. Use FRED's **Update** button and fill down the formulas in columns I, J, and K for each additional quarter. Of course, this also would be a straightforward additional assignment for students and may be fascinating depending on future Fed policy and rising federal funds rate.

5. Interest Rates and the Fisher Effect: This screencast compares bank prime lending rates and inflation. The relationship is not exact, but it is discernible from simple comparisons over time and on a scatter diagram. The explanation of why nominal interest and inflation rates move together relies on the Fisher Effect. The screencast explains how inflation erodes the value of money paid back and, therefore, the real interest rate can be approximated by subtracting the inflation rate from the nominal interest rate. Once this is understood, we can see how expected inflation must be incorporated into the nominal interest rate. The screencast concludes with the core lesson that it is unanticipated inflation that harms the economy.

   The task is an open-ended assignment in which the student has to construct various scenarios to demonstrate that it is not inflation per se that is dangerous to a lender but uncertainty in the inflation rate. A good answer should include a scenario showing that high inflation, if correctly forecasted (so expected inflation in cell M8 equals actual inflation in cell R8), does not affect the lender's real return. Another scenario should show that when M8 < R8, the lender's real return does not hit the target.

6. Exchange Rates: This screencast downloads and plots the Chinese yuan in terms of the U.S. dollar (which makes it obvious that China did not have a floating exchange rate), but then turns quickly to real effective exchange rates (REER). The primary objective is to convey how an index captures the movement of many prices. Along the way, the weights in the index (a function of the shares of trade with each country) provide an opportunity to show how Japan and China have flipped positions in terms of U.S. trade volume. REERs from the Fed and OECD are compared and shown to be fairly close. The recent history of the U.S. REER is briefly discussed, including the substantial decline in the past decade. The screencast concludes by claiming that central banks pay attention to exchange rates, but like inflation, it is difficult to show a correlation between money and exchange rate movements.

   The task has the student download and plot Canada's REER (FRED *Series ID CCRETT01CAA661N*). Since 2002, Canada's rapidly rising dollar (roughly 40% appreciation) is markedly different than the experience of the United States. Of course, the OECD provides REERs on many other countries. FRED *Series IDs* with 01 use CPI to measure inflation, while 02 signals inflation based on unit labor cost. Individual students or groups can be assigned countries and asked to present the results.

7. HP Filter: This final screencast shows how to apply the Hodrick–Prescott (HP) filter to M2. The mechanics of the algorithm are ignored, and the focus is on how to use Excel to produce a trend component to a cyclical time series. Care is needed when working with the HP user-defined function (available only when

the *Money.xls* workbook is open) because it is an array function. As stressed in the screencast, the CTRL-SHIFT-ENTER simultaneous keystroke combination is needed to properly enter array functions in Excel.

The task asks the student to apply the HP filter to real GDP. Naturally, any of the countless macro aggregates in FRED are grist for the HP mill. An interesting independent study project would be to replicate and extend Hodrick and Prescott (1997).

Although it can be assigned, this screencast is not meant to be part of the standard curriculum of an undergraduate intermediate macroeconomics course. It can be used, however, for a student writing a paper or a research assistant preparing data. It may also be appropriate for an advanced course or independent study project.

Conclusion

Money.xls uses FRED data to explore money supply; seigniorage; and inflation, interest, and exchange rates. The emphasis is on familiarity with historical trends and current conditions. For a money and banking course or if further emphasis on banking is needed, FRED has a great deal of information on reserves, balance sheet variables, and interest rates on commercial and Fed banks. For those who regularly visit http://www.federalreserve.gov and track H.4.1 or other releases, accessing these data via the FRED Excel add-in is a real time saver.

Since the focus is on data, little was said about monetary policy (although the monetarist experiment does feature prominently in the screencast on measuring money with MSI). See Lengwiler (2004) for an Excel-based monetary policy simulation game. Faced with a stream of stochastic shocks, the player is a central bank governor trying to steer the economy. The link to the files in the published paper no longer works, but the files are available at http://wwz.unibas.ch/fileadmin/wwz/redaktion/finance/personen/yvan/MoPoS/MoPoS.zip. The **Simulator** menu item in modern versions of Excel is listed in the **Add-Ins** tab.

In summary, while this chapter has downloaded data for a few fundamental macro variables (GDP, unemployment, inflation, and money), the screencasts have not come close to covering the full range of data in FRED. There are data on wages, capacity utilization, productivity, and much, much more. Because of its coverage and ease of use, the FRED Excel add-in is an excellent vehicle for student papers and projects. Even if some variables are missing, it is easy to augment the data set with variables from outside FRED. Perhaps best of all, the days of preparing data for students are long gone. They can and will use the FRED Excel add-in to obtain their own data and will then be able perform rudimentary analysis from within Excel.

Sources and Further Reading

The epigraph is from M. Friedman, *The Counter-Revolution in Monetary Theory: First Wincott Memorial Lecture* (1970), 24.

The Visual Basic code for the HP filter array function in *Money.xls* is from Yvan Lengwiler.

Barnett, W. 1984. "Recent Monetary Policy and the Divisia Monetary Aggregates." *American Statistician* 38, no. 3 (1984): 165–72, http://www.jstor.org/stable/2683646.

Barnett, W. 2011. *Getting It Wrong: How Faulty Monetary Statistics Undermine the Fed, the Financial System, and the Economy.* Kindle ed. MIT Press. MSI (Divisia) data for various countries are available at http://www.centerforfinancialstability .org/amfm.php.

Blanchard, O., and D. Johnson. 2013. *Macroeconomics.* 6th ed. Prentice Hall.

Cahill, M. 2006. "Estimating Key Macroeconomic Relationships at the Undergraduate Level: Taylor Rule and Okun's Law Examples." Paper presented at the American Economic Association annual meeting. http://college.holycross.edu/ faculty/mcahill/AEA2006/. See also http://serc.carleton.edu/econ/spreadsheets/ examples/42653.html.

Fischer, S. 1982. "Seigniorage and the Case for a National Money." *Journal of Political Economy* 90, no. 2: 295–313. http://www.jstor.org/stable/1830294.

Fisher, D. 2001. *Intermediate Macroeconomics: A Statistical Approach.* World Scientific.

Hodrick, R., and E. Prescott. 1997. "Postwar U.S. Business Cycles: An Empirical Investigation." *Journal of Money, Credit, and Banking* 29, no. 1: 1–16. http://www .jstor.org/stable/2953682.

Lengwiler, Y. 2004. "A Monetary Policy Simulation Game." *Journal of Economic Education* 35, no. 2: 175–83. http://www.jstor.org/stable/30042588.

Mandel, M. 1999. "Commentary: Rivers of Cash Won't Swamp the Economy." *BusinessWeek.* http://www.businessweek.com/stories/1999-03-07/ commentary-rivers-of-cash-wont-swamp-the-economy.

Mishkin, F. 2011. *Macroeconomics: Policy and Practice.* Prentice Hall.

5

The Keynesian Model

5.1

Introduction

The most significant theme emerging from the conference
was the desirability of adopting a single approach in
teaching the intermediate macroeconomics course, as
opposed to presenting numerous competing models.
– O. Homer Erekson, Prosper Raynold,
and Michael K. Salemi

Unlike growth theory, which enjoys strong consensus built around the Solow
Model, undergraduate teaching of short-run fluctuations is characterized by
a wide diversity of models and perspectives. This leads to an immediate and
critical pedagogical choice for an undergraduate macro course: reveal the
sharply conflicting views of various schools of macroeconomic thought or
teach a single, core model that is flexible enough to incorporate a range of
policy positions.

The ISLMADAS Model presented in this book and screencasts adheres
firmly to the latter option. As the epigraph to this chapter states, the single-
model approach was favored by the roughly one hundred macroeconomists
who gathered at a conference on the intermediate macroeconomics course in
1994. Although highlighting conflict can be exciting and intellectually stimulating, the costs in the classroom are quite high: "it is too expensive to teach
a new set of equations and the rules for manipulating them" (Erekson et al.
1996, 101). In a course with a few weeks on fluctuations, teaching more than
one model, such as Keynesian and real business cycle models, seems to err on
the side of breadth over depth. The likely outcome for an undergraduate student exposed to a blizzard of contradictory statements is a mix of confusion
and certainty that macroeconomists have no idea what they are taking about.

A Practical Pan-Macro Model

While not able to provide a taste of a modern macro model based on opti-
mizing agents, the ISLMADAS Model allows for a wide continuum of policy

possibilities. After all, the model says nothing about elasticities of various relationships nor speed of adjustment. With respect to policy, it easily reflects the views of leftist Keynesians and rightist monetarists and anyone in between, comfortably including the heterogeneous schools of modern macro under one umbrella. It gives, therefore, the undergraduate student a single model with which to intelligently discuss and interpret the news and policy debates of the day.

This applied orientation and policy flexibility is key to the ISLMADAS Model's amazing survival. Born as ISLM to convey inscrutable ideas presented in *The General Theory*, ADAS was grafted on in the 1970s as stagflation destroyed the Keynesian consensus. Colander (2003) offers a variety of reasons for the model's ability to withstand competitive threats (e.g., Romer 2000; Williamson 2011) and live on despite a complete lack of support from graduate curricula. Inertia plays a role, but its ability to deliver an optimal configuration of characteristics is critical:

> For the intermediate level student IS/LM is a nice pedagogical model; the level of math is about right, so that it challenges students – but not too much. It gives students something to learn that seems to have applications to policy and has, at least in the model, right or wrong answers. (Colander 2003, 6)

A short list of the ways in which the model gets it just right includes the following:

- Organizing Variables: From the initial goods market, with only consumption (C), investment (I), and government spending (G) equations determining equilibrium output (Y), to the full-blown ISLMADAS Model, clear demarcation of endogenous and exogenous variables is necessary to understanding how the model works. Students are able to repeatedly see how economists model and manipulate relationships among variables.
- Appreciating Model Building: The concept of a progression of models is a powerful unifying idea that must be emphasized. Just like the Solow Model, which is extended by population growth and technological change, the Keynesian Cross (goods market) is augmented with a money market to form ISLM and then further expanded to ISLMADAS. The screencasts highlight the attenuation of policy multipliers via feedback mechanisms as we endogenize the interest rate in ISLM and the price level in ISLMADAS.
- Interpreting and Computing Measures of Responsiveness: Working with the ISLMADAS family of models allows the student to see how different elasticities or parameter values produce different results. The effectiveness of monetary policy, for example, is not a binary response but a magnitude that depends on model parameters. This connects the model to the real world and estimation of parameter values.
- Reading Graphs: With graphs connected by shared common axes, the model often places exogenous variables on the y axis and endogenous variables on the x axis. This requires students to learn to read graphs properly. Furthermore, the model

generates comparative statics relationships (such as the IS, LM, and AD curves) that can be interpreted as magnets, equilibrium positions that attract points off these curves.

- Accessible Math: Finally, although not used at all in the screencasts, the mathematics of the ISLMADAS Model never rises above (admittedly tedious) algebra and the derivative for comparative statics. The workbooks contain step-by-step exposition of reduced-form solutions.

While the ISLMADAS Model is as simple as it gets (especially compared to a micro-founded model), it does require practice to achieve mastery. The lack of graduate training in the ISLMADAS Model poses a serious obstacle for newly minted PhDs assigned to teach intermediate macro. A decade ago, I offered a three-day NSF Chautauqua workshop on macroeconomics with Excel. The older participants struggled with the Solow Model, but the next day, we were all amused at how the roles were reversed. The younger participants really wrestled with the economics of the ISLMADAS Model, while the older folks were completely at ease. We agreed that the exposition in Excel gives a professor unfamiliar with ISLM and ADAS a quick way to grasp the fine points and properties of the model.

Ironically, teaching ISLMADS may fill a hole in the training of a modern macroeconomist by providing an easy way to communicate with nonexperts. This is why Krugman (2000, 41) argues for the preservation of little, simple models:

The point is not that these models are accurate or complete, or that they should be the only models used. Clearly they are incomplete, quite inadequate to examining some questions, and remain as full of *hoc* as ever. But they are easy to use, particularly on real-world policy questions, and often seem to give more or less the right answer.

The Downside of Teaching ISLMADAS

There are costs associated with using the ISLMADAS Model in the classroom. In addition to the weaknesses mentioned earlier (absence of microfoundations and complete irrelevance in the graduate school and professional academic arenas), the model suffers from confusing duplication once the price level is endogenized. This is not surprising given that the ISLM part of the model was created first, and much later the ADAS component was tacked on. While AD is simply equilibrium values of output given the price level, several different stories have been used to motivate the AS curve, only some of which are internally inconsistent with the unintended inventory changes version of supply in the goods market (Dutt 2002, 326). Mix in a healthy dose of poor naming and a tendency to show only the final ADAS graph and it is easy to see why Colander (1995) calls it "dirty pedagogy" (see also Kennedy's (1996) reply).

While these problems can be managed by a knowledgeable professor (although a few students may never really get that AD cannot be interpreted as a "giant demand curve"), there are two issues that are truly troubling. The first concerns the equilibration process. In the Keynesian Cross and ISLM models, there are reasonable explanations for how the system will reach its equilibrium position. Once P is endogenized, however, there is no story for how the model equilibrates. Mankiw (2013, 296) words it well when he says that AD and AS together "pin down the economy's price level and quantity of output." But the model has no clear explanation for exactly how a disequilibrium P, Y coordinate pair reaches equilibrium. The best we can say is that a disequilibrium point is *unsupportable* by the forces in the model.

The second fundamental problem with the ISLMADAS Model is that it is a completely static model and we are often interested in dynamics. For example, we want to know the effect of a policy move on inflation, but the most we can get from the ISLMADAS Model is a change in P in response to a shock, and we use the fact that the price level goes up or down as a proxy for a prediction about inflation or deflation. The same holds for changes in output: we can show that output will rise or fall, but the effect on economic growth (the percentage change in GDP over several time periods) is beyond the scope of the analysis. The model is about a single frame in a moving picture and has nothing much to say about evolution over time.

Conclusion

The unprecedented policy moves implemented by the Fed during the Great Recession exacerbate the difficult decisions to be made about content and method in the short-run fluctuations part of an intermediate macro course. Instructors should not respond to the fragmentation of macroeconomics by teaching a separate model for each school of thought or tailored to the hot topic of the day. For a recent review of the issues and trade-offs facing a professor teaching intermediate macro, see de Araujo et al. (2013).

A single approach, based on the ISLMADAS Model, is adopted here. This model has weaknesses, but its longevity reflects a fundamental capability to deliver appropriate content and skill development for undergraduate students. It offers a way to interpret real-world events and understand the mechanisms behind policy moves.

Like the Solow Model, the ISLMADAS Model requires a gradual rollout of ideas. Repetition and practice are necessary. The Excel implementation of the ISLMADAS Model is divided into four workbooks:

1. *KCross.xls* presents the familiar goods market equilibrium with Y as the sole endogenous variable in the Keynesian Cross (45 degree line) diagram.
2. *MoneyMarket.xls* provides a stepping-stone to endogenizing the interest rate. This workbook includes derivation of money demand via the Baumol–Tobin Model.

Class	Excel	Description	Highlights
1	*KCross.xls*	Introduction	Initial Y_e and shocking *PE*
2	*KCross.xls*	Comparative Statics	*G, T* Multipliers
3	*MoneyMarket.xls*	Equilibration	Money demand and supply establish equilibrium
4	*ISLM.xls*	Equilibration	The logic of the ISLM graph and solution
5	*ISLM.xls*	Comparative Statics	Shocks, multipliers, and policy
6	*ISLM.xls*	Comparative Statics	Elasticities of investment and money demand
7	*ISLM.xls.xls*	Comparative Statics	Deriving and understanding AD
8	*ISLMADAS.xls*	Equilibration	How the ISLM and ADAS graphs work together
9	*ISLMADAS.xls*	Comparative Statics	Shocks, policy, and multiplier attenuation
10	*ISLMADAS.xls*	Comparative Statics	Student presentations of historical episodes

Figure 5.1.1. Example curriculum for Keynesian Model coverage in a macro course.

3. *ISLM.xls* emphasizes the feedback mechanism from Y to money demand to the interest rate to investment and back to Y. It also explains how IS and LM are equilibrium positions for goods and money market whose intersection quickly shows the general equilibrium solution.
4. *ISLMADAS.xls* extends the model again, this time endogenizing the price level. It also includes short- and long-run aggregate supply, with SRAS a function of the expected price level.

These workbooks should be done in sequence, and only *MoneyMarket.xls* can be done in one day. All of the workbooks stress comparative statics and make it easy to compute policy multipliers. The algebra of the model is presented in separate sheets in the workbooks to enable a completely numerical and graphical exposition.

Many screencasts are included in these four Excel workbooks. A complete listing, organized in sequence within each workbook, is available from the *Course Materials* page at http://www.depauw.edu/learn/macroexcel/ screencasts. The website also has a full set of class handouts that can be edited and modified as needed. Figure 5.1.1 offers a starting point from which to build your curriculum for one-hour sessions in an intermediate macro course. It presumes familiarity with key macro variables. It also assumes further work, be it Phillips Curve or international extension, after this basic model is covered.

While the pace and content can be altered after the third class, it is a mistake to race too quickly through the *KCross.xls* and *MoneyMarket.xls* workbooks. The goods and money market are the two parts of this simple general equilibrium model that drive ISLM. Understanding how the two markets feed back upon each other is the absolute heart of the model.

While the main audience for the screencasts and Excel implementation of the Keynesian Model is an undergraduate student, these materials should prove helpful for the rookie professor expert in the ways of dynamic stochastic general equilibrium who is assigned to teach intermediate macroeconomics for the first time. The power of concrete, numerical presentation, live graphs, and video presentation will help overcome the yawning chasm between undergraduate and graduate macro models.

Sources and Further Reading

The epigraph is from O. Erekson, M. Salemi, and P. Raynold, "Pedagogical Issues in Teaching Macroeconomics," *Journal of Economic Education* 27, no. 2 (1996): 101, http://www.jstor.org/stable/1183017.

Colander, D. 1995. "The Stories We Tell: A Reconsideration of AS/AD Analysis." *Journal of Economic Perspectives* 9, no. 3: 169–88. http://www.jstor.org/stable/2138432.

Colander, D. 2003. "The Strange Persistence of the IS/LM Model." Economics Discussion Paper 03-07, Middlebury College. http://sandcat.middlebury.edu/econ/repec/mdl/ancoec/0307.pdf.

de Araujo, P., R. O'Sullivan, and N. B. Simpson. 2013. "What Should Be Taught in Intermediate Macroeconomics?" *Journal of Economic Education* 44, no. 1: 74–90. http://www.jstor.org/stable/41999255.

Dutt, A. K. 2002. "Aggregate Demand-Aggregate Supply Analysis: A History." *History of Political Economy* 34, no. 2: 321–63. http://muse.jhu.edu/journals/hpe/summary/v034/34.2dutt.html.

Kennedy, P. 1996. "Correspondence." *Journal of Economic Perspectives* 10, no. 3: 189–98. http://www.jstor.org/stable/2138529.

Krugman, P. 2000. "How Complicated Does the Model Have to Be?" *Oxford Review of Economic Policy* 16, no. 4: 33–42. doi:10.1093/oxrep/16.4.33.

Mankiw, N. 2013. *Macroeconomics*. 9th ed. Worth.

Romer, D. 2000. "Keynesian Macroeconomics without the LM Curve." *Journal of Economic Perspectives* 14, no. 2: 149–69. http://www.jstor.org/stable/2647100.

Williamson, S. D. 2011. *Macroeconomics*. 4th ed. Addison Wesley.

5.2

The Keynesian Cross: *KCross.xls*

> The income-expenditure model had its debut in Paul Samuelson's 1939 paper on the multiplier-accelerator interaction theory of the business cycle; in that paper Samuelson draws the consumption function in expenditure-income space and determines equilibrium in the goods market at the point of intersection of the C + I line (with investment given autonomously) with the 45° line. Although it is confined to a mere two pages in Samuelson's paper, in less than a decade this model became the backbone of Samuelson's 1948 principles text.
>
> – Amitava K. Dutt

Quick Summary

To access *KCross.xls*, visit

http://www.depauw.edu/learn/macroexcel/excelworkbooks/ISLMModel/KCross.xls

KCross.xls introduces the Keynesian Model. It emphasizes equilibration via unintended inventory changes and displays both the familiar income–expenditure diagram and savings equal to investment. The comparative statics properties of the model are explored, with G and T multipliers defined and computed.

Screencasts

- http://vimeo.com/econexcel/introkcross: introduction to the Keynesian Model stressing the concept of equilibrium and explaining how equilibrium Y is determined; shows how *Solver* can be used to find the equilibrium solution
- http://vimeo.com/econexcel/compstatickcross: shows how changes in exogenous variables affect equilibrium Y; the concept of elasticity is applied, and *Solver* is used to find the change in G needed to move the economy to full-employment Y

- http://vimeo.com/econexcel/multiplierkcross: explains the concept of a multiplier and how the G and T multipliers depend on the MPC

Introduction

Since the eventual goal is mastery and understanding of the ISLMADAS Model, it makes sense to begin carefully and slowly with the goods market and Keynesian Cross diagram. Unlike the Solow Model, students will have a passing acquaintance from introductory economics of Keynesian income determination, but there are subtle and fundamental issues that must be clearly explained to build a strong footing on which to erect a complicated superstructure.

Common Problems for Students

The dual nature of Y as output and income is a confusing concept that merits careful explanation. It is easy to see that consumption (C) is a function of income, and, with investment (I) and government spending (G) given, this makes planned expenditures (PE) also a function of income since $PE(Y) = C(Y) + I + G$. But things start to break down when we solve the model by setting $Y = PE(Y)$.

The crucial concept, of course, is that (assuming away depreciation) GDP and national income are the same. This enables the 45 degree line to translate income on the x axis to the same value of output on the y axis. The dual nature of Y, which can be conveyed by the idea of two sides of the same coin, explains how Y is output, the total amount of goods and services produced in a given time period, on the left-hand side of $Y = PE(Y)$; yet Y can be income determining a total amount of goods and services desired on the right-hand side.

Extra repetition is always a good idea when dealing with investment and government spending. Both are easily confused by popular uses of these terms. It is not easy for a student to keep in mind that a core component of investment is the purchase of new tools, plants, and equipment by firms nor to remember that transfer payments are not included in government spending.

Properly defining variables, especially the duality of GDP and income, goes a long way to helping students understand how the Keynesian Cross works. The *Intro* sheet lays out these definitions and offers a brief explanation of the intellectual obstacles Keynes overcame as he rejected prevailing, self-equilibrating theories. Do not underestimate the power of historical and biographical stories in attracting attention and helping students make sense of the Keynesian Model. Keynes was charismatic and could turn a phrase. It is easy to find video clips of his views on the gold standard and Great

Depression. Bringing him to life and explaining the rise of macroeconomics is an excellent use of class time. Heilbroner ([1953] 1999) remains a classic in this regard.

The Simple Keynesian Model of Income Determination

The structural equations of the model and single equilibrium condition are listed in the following and can be revealed in the *KCross.xls* workbook by clicking the `See Math` button from the *Model* sheet:

> Model Equations:
> $$C = C_0 + C_1(Y - T) \qquad \text{where } 0 < C_1 < 1$$
> $$I = I_0 + I_1 r \qquad\qquad\quad I_1 < 0$$
> $$G = G$$
> $$PE = C + I + G$$
>
> Equilibrium Condition:
> $$Y = PE$$

The model is implemented in Excel by listing the exogenous variables, labeling the endogenous variable (Y), and the equilibrium condition ($Y = PE$). The spreadsheet also includes a table of levels of Y and corresponding planned expenditures. The data from the table are used to create a Keynesian Cross diagram with an Investment $=$ Savings chart below it, as shown in Figure 5.2.1.

The equilibrium solution to this simple model can be found easily by using *Solver*, the table, or the charts. The table and charts clearly display disequilibrium values of Y and whether the economy will expand or contract as inventories signal over- or underproduction. The *Math* sheet also has a step-by-step derivation of the equilibrium solution.

A live version of the model, with the reduced-form expression entered as a formula for Y, is also available. This enables quick and easy comparative statics shifting of PE by simply changing an exogenous variable. The new PE line is red and the new Y_e is displayed. A button makes it easy to produce a new set of random parameters, for endless practice and homework problems. A particular configuration of exogenous variables can also be entered into cells B5:B11. Clicking the `Set Base` button will make this the benchmark case.

Finally, the workbook has a *Multiplier* sheet (displayed by clicking the `Multiplier` button from the *Live* sheet). It shows how repeated rounds of spending are summed to create a multiplicative effect on Y_e from a shock to G or T. Analysis of the multiplier is a thread throughout the four Excel workbooks. As

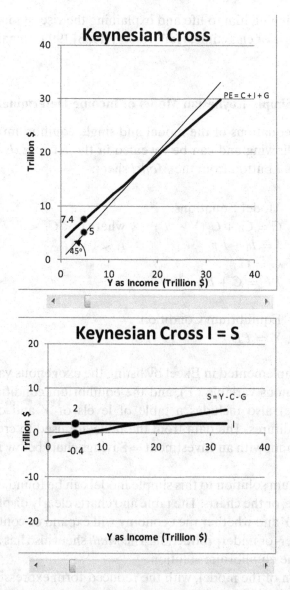

Figure 5.2.1. The simple planned expenditure model.
Source: Model sheet in *KCross.xls.*

the model is extended to ISLM and then ISLMADAS, the student will see
that the magnitude of the multiplier falls.

Screencasts and Tasks

1. Introduction to the Keynesian Cross: This screencast provides an overview of the
   Keynesian Model before introducing the Keynesian Cross. It stresses the difference between long-run analysis and short-run economic fluctuations using the

stylized graph in the *Intro* sheet. The screencast continues by reviewing the cells and buttons on the sheet, then focuses on the equilibration process. It connects equilibration in supply and demand (which presumably is well understood by most students) to the Keynesian Cross diagram. Using a concrete example, referring to numbers on the sheet, it walks through disequilibrium values of Y above and below the equilibrium solution, stressing how changes in inventories will drive the system to equilibrium. Any gap between actual GDP on the 45 degree line and planned expenditures on the PE line must be handled by changes in inventories. It is these unintended inventory accumulations and decumulations that drive the system to equilibrium. After showing how *Solver* can be used to find Y_e, the screencast concludes by displaying the $I = S$ version of the model and pointing out that, in the future, the IS curve will represent equilibrium in the goods market.

The task follows the screencast closely. The student is asked to create his or her own economy (using the random parameters button) and then choose an initial $Y > Y_e$. To complete the task, the student must explain how the model will equilibrate. This reinforces how equilibration works in the Keynesian Cross by having the student explain the process in his or her own words.

2. Comparative Statics with the Keynesian Cross: The second screencast uses the *Live* sheet to change the consumption intercept and slope (*MPC*), pointing out that the slope has a more powerful effect on output than the intercept. It uses the language of elasticity but does not actually do any elasticity computations (which would be a good additional task or demonstration in class). After a brief Excel lesson on concatenating cells, the screencast shows how to use *Solver* to find the value of G that pushes Y_e to a given full-employment level.

The task mirrors the screencast and has the student double the interest rate in an economy with randomly generated parameters. Once again, the student explains in his or her own words what effect this has on Y_e (it must fall) and why (because investment must decrease as r rises).

3. G and T Multipliers in the Keynesian Cross: The final screencast is devoted to the multiplier. After defining the multiplier as a factor of proportionality, the hidden *Multiplier* sheet is revealed and used to explain how repeated rounds of spending are the source of the multiplicative effect of an initial increase in G. The concrete example makes clear that the sum of the infinite series converges. A review of the T multiplier stresses why it is weaker than changing G and how both multipliers depend on the *MPC*. The screencast concludes by setting $MPC = 0.5$ and using the ⌞Set Base⌟ button to create a new benchmark case. Using the Keynesian Cross diagram, it is easy to see that changes in G are less powerful because *PE* is much flatter than it was before.

The final task is more difficult than the first two because it asks the student to shock both G and T by the same amount to figure out the value of the balanced budget multiplier. No matter the configuration of exogenous variables, the balanced budget multiplier is exactly 1 because adding the two multipliers yields

$$\frac{\Delta Y_e}{\Delta G} + \frac{\Delta Y_e}{\Delta T} = \frac{1}{1 - MPC} - \frac{MPC}{1 - MPC} = 1.$$

In terms of the *Multiplier* sheet, an increase in G and T by the same amount cancels all of the repeated rounds of spending, except the initial one.

A sharp student might note that this result is impractical. After all, any level of Y can be easily reached by an appropriate, equal change in G and T. This suggests an optimal policy of simultaneously raising G and T infinitely. Such a comment should trigger a discussion of the limits of modeling.

Conclusion

The *KCross.xls* workbook is a gentle introduction to the Keynesian Model. Important concepts include the notion that equilibrium output is determined by demand for output from consumers, firms, and governments (which is called "planned expenditure" instead of "aggregate demand," to lessen confusion when we derive AD as a function of P). Comparative statics and multipliers are discussed to place these foundational concepts as high-priority items.

Intermediate-level students will have some familiarity with the model from a previous course, but providing a historical perspective on the model, clearly defining the variables and functions, and explaining how the equilibration process works is plenty of material for one class period. This leaves comparative statics and multipliers for a second day.

The *Intro* sheet prints on six landscaped pages for convenient use as a handout during a class lecture or reading assignment. Other class handouts as easily modifiable Word documents are available at http://www.depauw.edu/learn/macroexcel. The introduction to the Keynesian Cross handout includes instructions on using FRED to get data on the GDP gap and unemployment to connect equilibrium output to the unemployment rate.

Sources and Further Reading

The epigraph is from A. Dutt, "Aggregate Demand-Aggregate Supply Analysis: A History," *History of Political Economy* 34, no. 2 (2002): 330. This paper not only traces the history of the ISLM-ADAS Model through principles and intermediate macro textbooks but also makes clear how to avoid inconsistency from using two supply stories when teaching the model.

Heilbroner, R. (1953) 1999. *The Worldly Philosophers: The Lives, Times, and Ideas of the Great Economic Thinkers.* Rev. 7th ed. Simon and Schuster.

5.3

The Money Market: *MoneyMarket.xls*

> The bad news is that we have just been through a once-in-hundred-year credit tsunami that has had a devastating impact on the economy that will last for years to come. The good news is that macro/monetary economists and central bankers do not have to go back to the drawing board and throw out all that they have learned over the last forty years.
> – Frederic S. Mishkin

Quick Summary

To access *MoneyMarket.xls*, visit

http://www.depauw.edu/learn/macroexcel/excelworkbooks/ISLMModel/MoneyMarket.xls

MoneyMarket.xls provides a quick explanation of the equilibrium interest rate (r) that is produced by money demand and supply. It also uses the Baumol–Tobin Model to explain why money demand is a function of the interest rate and income.

Screencasts

- http://vimeo.com/econexcel/mmintro: introduces the money market and uses Excel's *Solver* to find the equilibrium interest rate
- http://vimeo.com/econexcel/mmcs: does comparative statics in the money market by exploring the effect on the equilibrium interest rate when changing the money supply
- http://vimeo.com/econexcel/mmmoneydemand: uses a Baumol–Tobin Model to derive money demand from a comparative statics analysis (using the *Scenario Comp Statics* add-in)

Introduction

This workbook is a stepping-stone on the way to the ISLM Model. Instead of an exogenously given interest rate, money demand and money supply (real balances) determine the equilibrium interest rate, which is then fed into the investment demand function to determine the level of investment. To help students understand money demand, a Baumol–Tobin Model is implemented. The explicit display of a money management optimization problem is an excellent way to imprint the concept of money demand.

Common Problems for Students

Money is undoubtedly one of the most confusing variables in economics. In the Keynesian Model, it is easily tangled with government spending. After all, both are in units of currency and used as policy tools. For the same reasons, students mix up money with income and wealth. Distinctions between stocks and flows are too subtle to be noticed. It may be worthwhile to review or assign the *Money.xls* workbook to remind students of basic monetary concepts.

Beyond these fundamental definitional problems and the need to highlight getting the variables exactly right, there is the issue of the money market itself (by which is meant a chart with demand for and supply of money, not a real-world financial market for short-term securities). As pointed out in the *Intro* sheet, this is not your standard shortage and surplus equilibration process. What is really going on is that equilibration is driven by the bond market (the alternative, interest-bearing asset to money). There really are shortages and surpluses in the bond market that drive the interest rate to its equilibrium position, and this is reflected in the money market by the intersection of money demand and money supply.

The Money Market Model

As the *Intro* sheet explains, a simplifying assumption is that the central bank exactly controls the money supply. Real balances are used in anticipation of flexible prices in later models. The *Intro* sheet also points out that varying prices causes a complication in that money demand depends on the nominal interest rate, while investment (and, later on, the IS curve) depends on the real interest rate. This is all swept under the rug.

Money demand is initially a function solely of the interest rate (see the *Lr* sheet) but quickly extends to include income (in the *LrY* sheet). The *L* represents liquidity preference, and this term is used synonymously with money demand. This connects the LM curve to the money market in later models:

Model Equations:
$$L = L_0 + L_r r + L_Y Y \quad \text{where } L_r < 0 \text{ and } L_Y \geq 0$$
$$M^s = \frac{M}{P}$$

Equilibrium Condition:
$$L = M^s$$

A hidden *Algebra* sheet can be revealed by a button click to display the step-by-step algebraic solution, but the screencast uses *Solver* to find the equilibrium interest rate and a live sheet (with the reduced-form equilibrium solution entered as a formula) to do comparative statics.

Click the [Origins of L] button in row 65 of the *Intro* sheet to reveal the hidden *L* sheet. This has an implementation of the Baumol–Tobin Model, with a brief description of the model. *Solver* can be used to find the optimal number of trips to the bank and, therefore, average money holdings. By changing the interest rate and income, the money demand function can be derived. Scroll down to row 100 to see a calculus-based derivation.

Screencasts and Tasks

1. Introduction to the Money Market: The first screencast begins by pointing out that the money market is the financial counterpart to the goods market and that the two are connected by the investment function. It then stresses that the equilibration process is played out in the bond market, but the intersection of money demand and supply does reflect the equilibrium interest rate. *Solver* is used to find the equilibrium solution in the *Lr* sheet, and then the focus moves to the *LrY* sheet, where income is added to the money demand function. Finally, a version of the model with the reduced-form solution entered as a formula in the *LrYLive* sheet is reviewed.

   The task asks the student to explore the effect of an increase in income on the equilibrium interest rate. The easiest way to answer this question is to use the *LrYLive* sheet because changing cell B12 from 17 to 20 immediately updates the chart and shows that the rightward shift in money demand leads to an increase in the equilibrium interest rate.

2. Money Market Comparative Statics: The second screencast shows two ways to do comparative statics. The first uses the *LrYLive* sheet to show how an increase in the money supply lowers interest rates and stimulates the economy. The second way uses the button. This is an Excel add-in (available freely on the website), but it has also been embedded in the workbook. Clicking on the [Scenario Comp Statics] button pops up a dialog box in which the user enters information and a macro produces scenarios that are displayed in a new sheet. Although not done in the screencast, showing

students how to create a chart of the equilibrium interest rate as a function of the money supply and computing elasticities would be worthwhile.

   The task requires some thought and foreshadows future work using the interest rate elasticity of money demand. The student must interpret the question and use the scroll bar to set the *r* elasticity of *L* to zero. This makes money demand nearly vertical (since the interest rate, the exogenous variable, is on the *y* axis). Clearly tiny increases in the money supply will now produce big changes in the equilibrium interest rate, making Fed policy extremely powerful, ceteris paribus.

3. Deriving the Money Demand Function: The final screencast is a great way to help students really connect the dots on money demand. By explicitly modeling the trade-off between holding cash and earning interest with bank deposits, the core logic of money demand is made clear. *Solver* is used to find optimal money holding with a 10% interest rate. To determine the effect of changes in the interest rate on money demand, the [Scenario Comp Statics] button is copied and pasted on the *L* sheet and used to derive optimal money demand as a function of the interest rate.

   The task is a modified version of the screencast in which the student shows the effect of income on optimal money holding. As *Y* rises, so does the quantity of money demanded. A calculus-based version of this problem can be assigned by asking students to find the derivative of the reduced-form solution of optimal money (scroll down to row 100 of the *L* sheet) with respect to *Y*.

Conclusion

This workbook is quite compact and can be delivered in a single class period. The primary ideas are straightforward and accessible. The *Intro* sheet prints on four landscaped pages, and class handouts are available at http://www .depauw.edu/learn/macroexcel. Armed with the notion that the money market establishes an equilibrium interest rate, we are poised to present the ISLM Model.

   In terms of Excel, the workbook utilizes *Solver* and Excel's scenarios to do comparative statics. Numerical methods for comparative statics are an extremely effective way to convey the logic of the economic way of thinking. The *MoneyMarket.xls* workbook uses the [Scenario Comp Statics] button twice to reinforce this approach.

Sources and Further Reading

The epigraph is from F. S. Mishkin, "Monetary Policy Strategy: Lessons from the Crisis," Working Paper 16755 (NBER, 2011), 47, http://www.nber.org/papers/ w16755.

5.4

The ISLM Model: *ISLM.xls*

> Paul Krugman recently wondered how many
> macroeconomists still believe in the IS-LM model. The
> answer is probably that most do, but many of them
> probably do not know it well enough to tell.
> – Olivier Blanchard

Quick Summary

To access *ISLM.xls*, visit

http://www.depauw.edu/learn/macroexcel/excelworkbooks/ISLMModel/ISLM.xls

ISLM.xls implements the ISLM Model with an initial emphasis on the idea of a feedback mechanism and stresses the equilibration process. This workbook also enables a variety of comparative statics and multiplier analyses. Exploration of the properties of the model under various parameter values and elasticities is emphasized.

Screencasts

There are eleven screencasts organized into three groups:

Group 1: The first four screencasts are focused on the initial equilibrium and how it is obtained.

- http://vimeo.com/econexcel/islmintro: introduces the ISLM Model with a no-feedback version of the model where income does not affect money demand; when we make money demand a function of income, in the next screencast, the power and effectiveness of the IS and LM curves become immediately clear
- http://vimeo.com/econexcel/islmequilibration: shows how the goods and money markets are interconnected and how the intersection of IS and LM reveals the general equilibrium solution

- http://vimeo.com/econexcel/islmassetmarket: shows how an ISLM Model with asset market equilibration works by displaying an economy crawling along the LM curve to its equilibrium solution
- http://vimeo.com/econexcel/islmstability: shows how the slopes of the IS and LM curves determine if the equilibrium solution is stable under a cobweb equilibration process

Group 2: The next three screencasts are concerned with the mechanics of the model itself and how it functions.

- http://vimeo.com/econexcel/islmderive: derives the IS and LM curves as equilibrium solutions – for IS, Y_e given r, and for LM, r_e given Y
- http://vimeo.com/econexcel/islmshifting: shows how to correctly shift curves depending on the placement of the exogenous variable; emphasizes that for shocks that do not affect the slope, the IS curve shifts left and right, while the LM curve shifts up and down
- http://vimeo.com/econexcel/islmcrowdingout: how multipliers are attenuated (lessened) when the model is extended because investment is crowded out as interest rates rise in response to attempts to stimulate the economy

Group 3: The final four screencasts are devoted to the comparative statics properties of the model, including applications and analysis of fiscal and monetary policy.

- http://vimeo.com/econexcel/islmfluctuations: shows how the ISLM Model can be used to explain economic fluctuations; in essence, booms and busts are driven by shocks that affect demand and drive equilibrium output and unemployment
- http://vimeo.com/econexcel/islmpolicy: shows how fiscal policy (G and T) and monetary policy (M^s) can be used to move the economy to its full-employment, potential GDP position
- http://vimeo.com/econexcel/islmfedpowerless: shows how the liquidity trap, zero bound, and inelastic investment demand can short-circuit the monetary transmission mechanism, leaving the Fed unable to use traditional monetary policy to steer the economy
- http://vimeo.com/econexcel/islmderivingad: derives aggregate demand (AD) from the ISLM graph and shows how AD shifts left and right as G, T, and M^s change

Introduction

The *ISLM.xls* workbook presents the ISLM Model in a clearly organized spreadsheet that includes goods and money market charts along with the ISLM graph. The emphasis is on understanding the linkages among graphs and variables, how the model behaves under different parameter values and elasticities, and how to use the model to interpret events of the day and appropriate policy responses.

The sheets are designed to be flexible and allow the user to easily draw random parameter values or apply a particular configuration. By clicking the Make Base button, you make the existing parameters the benchmark case. Click the Reset to Base button after changing parameters to return to your benchmark case. The Intial button returns the original parameter values. The buttons surrounding the charts are used to center and improve the display produced by a new parameter set.

Common Problems for Students

Like supply and demand, ISLM is trivial in the sense that the answer is obviously at the intersection of the two curves. There is no other interesting, competing point on the graph, so this has to be the answer. But underlying this superficial observation about the equilibrium solution is a complicated story and set of relationships that can be confusing to students. To assess understanding, the critical question is, Why is the intersection of IS and LM the solution? The pedagogical holy grail of the ISLM Model is to have a student master the mechanics of the model so that news events can be interpreted and policy moves understood.

Textbooks present the ISLM Model by first deriving the IS and LM curves. Although a logical way to teach the model, it completely misses the point of the cleverness inherent in the ISLM graph and does not give the student a chance to appreciate the difficulty of finding the general equilibrium solution in a system with two endogenous variables that depend upon each other. Introducing the model by deriving IS and LM is like teaching someone how to drive a car by showing the person schematics and explaining how a car is built. Everyone learns to drive by actually driving and repeated practice.

In my experience, ISLM is better taught by first showing how the model equilibrates and how the intersection of IS and LM determines the solution. After the student develops an awareness of the way the IS and LM curves work and display the equilibrium solution, the IS and LM curves can be derived. This gives the student a much clearer picture of how the IS and LM curves capture equilibrium in the two underlying goods and money markets.

Explicitly focusing on equilibration from the very beginning also provides a laser-like focus on the most fundamental part of the model – the feedback mechanism from income to money demand. Once the student grasps that changes in income in the goods market shift money demand and interest rates, which then affect investment and planned expenditures, the logic of the model is laid bare.

A great advantage of the Excel implementation of the model is how easily it enables comparison of the model under varying parameter values and elasticities. In a book, a graph that compares, for example, elastic and inelastic investment demand is difficult to follow because the student must reconstruct the argument by imagining how the various curves shift as the elasticity changes. Excel has two powerful advantages over the printed book: (1) the student controls the elasticity, triggering the shifts and movements along curves, and (2) the display eliminates the need to imagine – the consequences of a shock are clearly presented. Thus, a student can explore the properties of the model by moving scroll bars to apply different elasticities and connecting the effect of, for example, a flat money demand to the LM curve. This is a major improvement over rote memorization of how the model looks under different parameter values.

Another source of confusion that is rarely dealt with involves reading graphs. The ISLM Model strategically flips the axes, sometimes putting endogenous variables on the x axis and exogenous variables on the y axis (e.g., Y and r for the IS curve). The workbook and screencasts explain this point and provide clear instruction on how to read a graph. In addition, the interpretation of the IS and LM curves as magnets, attracting points off the curves, is a potent metaphor to help students understand how ISLM works.

The ISLM Model

As usual, the *Intro* sheet lays out the primary ideas. It explains the concept of a feedback mechanism and that we are dealing with a general equilibrium system with two endogenous variables:

> Model Equations:
> $C = C_0 + C_1(Y - T)$ where $0 < C_1 < 1$
> $I = I_0 + I_1 r$ $I_1 < 0$
> $G = G$
> $PE = C + I + G$
> $L = L_0 + L_r r + L_Y Y$ where $L_r < 0$ and $L_Y \geq 0$
> $M^s = \frac{M}{P}$
> Equilibrium Conditions:
> $Y = PE$
> $L = M^s$

A hidden *Math* sheet can be revealed by a button click from the *ISLM* sheet (near cell L1) to display the step-by-step algebraic solution, but the screencasts make no mention of the analytical solution. In a nutshell, the screencasts explain the model by first considering a version with no feedback mechanism, that is, $L_Y = 0$. In this case, changes in income have no effect on money demand, and there is only a one-way interaction from r to Y. In other words, a shock in the goods market that increases Y has no impact on interest rates or investment. With $L_Y = 0$, LM is horizontal.

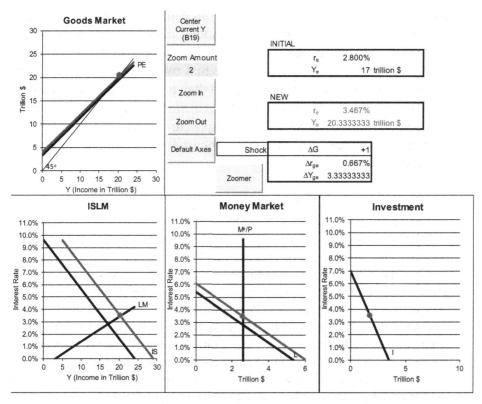

Figure 5.4.1. An increase in G in the ISLM Model.
Source: ISLMCS sheet in *ISLM.xls*.

Allowing income to affect money demand, $L_Y > 0$, gives rise to the conventional ISLM Model with an upward sloping LM curve. The screencast describes this as having a feedback mechanism from income to money demand. A shock in the goods market that increases Y will shift money demand right, increasing r, decreasing I, decreasing PE, and, therefore, feeding back into and lowering Y relative to the no-feedback case. Figure 5.4.1 shows the display after an increase in government spending.

The *Math* sheet has a convenient set of cells where various parameter configurations can be entered to create lecture, homework, or exam questions. For a more mathematically sophisticated presentation, scroll down to the bottom of the *Math* sheet to see a solution via linear algebra. Excel has rudimentary matrix multiplication capability, and this is a nice example of how matrix computations can be used to solve a model.

Screencasts and Tasks

There is a lot of material here, and some professors may not wish to go into as great a depth as presented in the eleven screencasts. It is helpful to know when deciding what to cover that there are three main parts: (1) understanding equilibrium, (2) the mechanics of the model, and (3) comparative statics (which is essentially how policy is interpreted and applied). With a tight time constraint, it would make sense to use the first two screencasts (since they explain the essential logic of the model) and then pick from each of the other two parts. See Figure 5.1.1 and visit the *Course Materials* page at http://www.depauw.edu/learn/macroexcel for an example curriculum.

Group 1: The first four screencasts are focused on the initial equilibrium and how it is obtained.

1A. Introduction to the ISLM Model: The first step is to present the no-feedback version of the model. In cell F21 of the *NoFeedback* sheet, the unidirectional chain of events is displayed: $r \to I \to PE \to Y$. Changes in r affect Y, but Y does not affect r because $L_Y = 0$. By clicking the $\boxed{\text{Random Initial r, Y}}$ button, a disequilibrium combination of r and Y is displayed on the sheet, and the voice-over explains how we get to equilibrium by a two-step process: first, we clear the money market (using the $\boxed{\text{Clear Money Market}}$ button), which gives the level of investment at the equilibrium r, and then we find equilibrium Y in the goods market (via the $\boxed{\text{Clear Goods Market}}$ button). After reminding the student that the G and T multipliers were 5 and -4, respectively, the money supply is increased by \$1 trillion, and we see that the M^s multiplier is 2.5. The screencast shows how the $\boxed{\text{Intial}}$ button resets the parameter values to their initial positions and enters the reduced-form solution for r and Y. This makes comparative statics a snap. The screencast concludes by describing how the multiplier can be used to drive the economy to a given level of output.

The associated task in the *ToDo* sheet is straightforward. The student clicks the $\boxed{\text{Random Parameters}}$ button and computes the three multipliers. Checking student answers for any parameter configuration is easy because cells J38:J40 in the *Math* sheet have formulas for the no-feedback multipliers.

1B. Understanding Equilibrium in the ISLM Model: This critical screencast shows how the feedback mechanism triggers looping from goods market to money market and back again, until the system settles down to its general equilibrium position. The demonstration begins by manually entering initial r and Y values in cells B18 and B19, respectively, of the *ISLM* sheet. (Manually entering values may be helpful for an in-class example or as an extra assignment.) After clearing the money market, clicking on the button to clear the goods market does not end the story, as it did in the *NoFeedback* sheet. The new equilibrium level of income shifts money demand and knocks the money market out of equilibrium. Instead of oscillating forever, repeated clicking of the two buttons to clear the two markets makes clear that the system actually settles down to a unique and stable equilibrium position (given the initial parameter configuration). Clicking the $\boxed{\text{Show ISLM}}$ button (which toggles showing and hiding the chart) displays the ISLM graph and makes clear that the intersection of IS and LM locates the equilibrium solution. The screencast uses language of being "off the curve" to connect the notion of disequilibrium in the underlying market to the IS and

LM curves. This is followed by highlighting that points are attracted to the IS and LM curves and that thinking of them as magnets is a great way to convey how IS and LM work. The video concludes by animating the process with the `Play ▶` button. (This button is an excellent device for explaining equilibration while lecturing.)

The task is to explain why $L_Y = 0$ is so critical to the operation of the model with a randomly generated economy. This forces the student to put the ideas in the first two screencasts on the feedback mechanism into his or her own words. Student answers to this question can reveal problems in understanding the model. As described in the task, clicking **Yes** to the dialog box that pops up when the `Random Parameters` button is clicked is necessary to make sure that the two models in the *NoFeedback* and *ISLM* sheets yield identical, initial equilibrium positions (the macro adjusts the money demand intercept after setting $L_Y = 0$ in the *NoFeedback* sheet).

1C. Asset Market Equilibration in the ISLM Model: This screencast points out that the idea that the goods and money markets are going to take turns equilibrating is nonsensical. If one assumes that financial markets clear more quickly and are always in equilibrium, then the equilibration process is different. From any dis-equilibrium coordinate position, the point will be strongly attracted to the LM curve (the screencast calls it a "black hole bar magnet") and then crawl along the LM curve to the general equilibrium intersection of IS and LM. The end of the screencast points out that the model does not have the dynamics well worked out, and we study equilibration to understand how the model works.

The task has the student generate a random economy and explain, in his or her own words, how the economy would reach equilibrium via the asset market story. As with the second task, it is easy to see from a student's answer if the student is confused and where he or she may need help.

1D. The Stability of Cobweb Equilibration: The final screencast in this group is rather advanced. The basic idea is to show that parameter values determine whether the cobweb equilibration process is stable. As mentioned in the screen-cast, this may not have much real-world application, but it does help students understand how IS and LM work. A productive computer lab group or class assignment is to have students generate economies and compare them. The group or class can try to figure out how likely we are to get stable or unstable economies.

Students may wonder why we take the reciprocal of the LM slope when form-ing the stability condition. This is needed to make them comparable because the IS curve is "drawn backward." By looking at the values of the IS and LM inter-cepts in the cells above the ratio of the slopes, one can see that the IS intercept is actually the x axis intercept. The Excel workbook flips the LM slope to make them comparable, but it could have been done this way: (1/IS slope)/LM slope. Either way, it is the ratio of the slopes that determines stability when you cob-web equilibrate, and a steeper IS than LM is needed for stability. Intuitively, if the slopes are the same, the cobweb would be a rectangle, neither converging nor diverging from the intersection.

The task is based on the student replicating the analysis in the screencast with a random economy. Alternating goods and money market clearing should produce a result that agrees with cell G38.

Group 2: The next three screencasts are concerned with the mechanics of the model itself and how it functions.

2A. Deriving the IS and LM Curves: The first screencast derives the IS and LM curves. The *NoFeedback* sheet is used to compute Y_e for different values of *r*. Drawing a chart of the data produces the IS curve. The SERIES formula is edited to flip the axes, putting the interest rate, which is the exogenous variable, on the *y* axis. The video explains that to put both IS and LM on the same graph, one of them has to be flipped. Attention then turns to the LM curve, which is derived in the *ISLM* sheet by tracking equilibrium *r* given *Y*. The screencast concludes by clicking the [Show ISLMCS] button, which reveals a new sheet that is set up for quick comparative statics analysis and has scroll bars to adjust the elasticities of money demand and the investment function. Manipulating these scroll bars provides powerful visuals and helps students understand how the model works. The video discusses the effect of perfectly inelastic investment demand (which makes IS vertical) and then shows how a perfectly inelastic money demand function makes LM vertical.

The task asks the student to create a random economy and work out the implications of a perfectly elastic investment demand function for Fed policy. No matter the parameters, as the interest rate elasticity of investment rises (in absolute value), the IS curve will get flatter. Thus, the answer to the question is that monetary policy will be more effective, ceteris paribus, the more interest rate elastic the investment function, because a given change in *r* will have a bigger effect on *I* and, eventually, Y_e.

2B. Exactly Correctly Shifting: The second screencast in this group is nonstandard but important. Economists often flip axes (as in micro supply and demand curves and the IS curve), yet we do not explain the implications of this to our students. Instead, we adopt hazy language, for example, "shifts in or out," and sometimes even draw diagonal arrows to show a shift. This is, to be blunt, a ridiculous state of affairs. In fact, there are clear, logical rules for how to read a graph and shift a curve. This screencast attempts to explicitly state these rules and show students how to read a graph.

It begins by showing a shift in the LM curve from a shock to the money demand intercept in the *ISLMCS* sheet. LM shifts up, PE shifts down, and money demand shifts right. Increasing the investment intercept shifts PE up, IS right, money demand right, and investment demand right. The rule is to shift the curve from the perspective of the exogenous variable. The [Show Shifting] button reveals the *Shifting* sheet, which contains a detailed explanation of how to read graphs and shift curves. Scroll down to the bottom of this sheet to see a nice visualization of how difficult it is to interpret shifting curves. The screencast concludes by pointing out that the shifts in IS and LM correspond to how points off the curves are attracted – left or right for IS and up or down for LM.

The task asks students to search the Web for images of shifting IS or LM curves that are wrong. This works well with class discussions or group work. Students easily find images of IS and LM shifts that are incorrect, given the model implemented in Excel (which is a way to be charitable on this point – the model used by someone claiming that the LM shifts left or right may be different).

2C. Attenuation and Crowding Out: The final screencast in this group shows how crowding out produces smaller multipliers. It compares the *G* multiplier of 5 in the *NoFeedback* sheet to the *G* multiplier of 3.33 in the *ISLMCS* sheet. The increase in *G* caused *Y* to increase, but this increased money demand and the interest rate rose, crowding out investment. The screencast shows a second way to explain this by copying the parameters from the *NoFeedback* sheet to the *ISLMCS* sheet. With $L_Y = 0$, the LM curve is horizontal, and there is no crowding out because the interest rate stays constant. The screencast emphasizes that this is a common result – as the model is extended, multipliers shrink. It also demonstrates that the money supply multiplier is also smaller when LM is upward sloping, and for the same reason: interest rates rise as money demand increases.

Since the screencast worked with *G* and M^s, the task asks the student to explore the effect of an upward sloping LM on the *T* multiplier. The student will find that it also is attenuated. Another assignment could involve confirming that the direction of the shock, up or down, does not change the basic result. In other words, a decrease in *G* will lead to a smaller reduction in equilibrium *Y* when LM is upward sloping. A difficult homework or exam question would ask the student to define and explain *crowding in*.

Group 3: The final four screencasts are devoted to the comparative statics properties of the model, including applications and analysis of fiscal and monetary policy.

3A. Explaining Fluctuations with ISLM: The first screencast presents the Keynesian view of economic fluctuations as the product of demand shocks. Three ways of doing comparative statics are reviewed. The first way is the simplest: change a parameter in the *ISLMCS* sheet and the graphs update to display the new solution with red lines. The screencast demonstrates how the consumption intercept might increase with a stock market boom or fall as housing prices collapsed in the Great Recession. It points out that the feedback mechanism provides an automatic stabilizer to the economy, mitigating the effects of a negative shock. The second way explores the effect of changes in the *MPC* using the <kbd>Scenario Comp Statics</kbd> button. The last approach connects the model to the real world. A chart of real *Y*, *C*, and *I* for the United States since 1929 (located near cell E50 of the *ISLMCS* sheet) shows actual, historical fluctuations. The formula = RAND()*0.1 + 3.5 transforms the investment intercept parameter into a stochastic variable.

Pressing F9 produces a new value and a new equilibrium solution. The Track Eq
button recalculates the workbook (drawing a new random investment intercept)
100 times, adds a 3% growth rate after each draw, and displays the results in a
new sheet. Since the fluctuations are too small, more noise is added by modifying the formula so that RAND() is multiplied by 1. This simulation (available
by unhiding the *S3A* sheet) shows more variability, but by comparing it to the
actual data, we can see that consumption is too variable and investment is not
volatile enough. In addition, we are not getting several periods of downturn followed by extended booms. In other words, there is no serial correlation in the
simulated data. The analysis does convey, however, the essential heart of the
Keynesian story: economic fluctuations are caused by a series of random shocks
to aggregate demand, especially investment.

The associated task is open ended and difficult. The student is invited to
try adding randomness to another exogenous variable. The results depend on
exactly how much noise is injected and which variable is highlighted. The assignment can be made easier by giving an explicit set of instructions. For example,
the task could be to randomize the *MPC* with the formula $= \text{RAND()}^*.05 +$
3.5, run a simulation, and evaluate the results.

3B. Macro Policy Tools in the ISLM Model: This screencast shows how policy tools
can be used to manage and manipulate the economy. After reviewing the simple
logic of how taxes affect *C*, the money supply affects *I* (through *r*), and *G* directly
affects planned expenditures, the three policy tools are demonstrated via a concrete example with full-employment *Y* = $20 trillion. The screencast shows how
to work out the needed change in *G* to reach potential GDP by using the *G* multiplier. It then uses *Solver* to find the appropriate tax cut. Finally, increases in the
money supply are tested on the *ISLMCS* sheet to place the economy at the target level of *Y*. The video concludes by pointing out that policy in the real world
is obviously more complicated. We do not know the parameters of the economy,
so we do not have the information needed to fine-tune the economy. If investment demand is more elastic, then an increase in *G* will cause greater crowding
out, and a bigger stimulus will be needed. We also do not know where the economy is headed. The purpose of the ISLM Model is to enable us to interpret and
understand how policy impacts the economy.

The task asks the student to generate a random economy and show how the
three policy tools can be used to reach a full-employment level of output that is
10% greater than equilibrium *Y*. It is fairly easy to see if the student understands
what is going on, but, if needed, student parameter configurations can be entered
(or copied and pasted if the file can be accessed electronically) to check answers.

3C. Breaking the Monetary Transmission Mechanism: This screencast focuses on
monetary policy and how it can break down. Three situations are considered: (1)
a liquidity trap, (2) hitting the zero lower bound, and (3) an extremely inelastic
investment demand. By using the scroll bar to make money demand extremely
elastic, we can show that changes in the money supply will not change the interest rate. The screencast mentions quantitative easing as an innovative solution
after the Fed hit the zero lower bound. Finally, the video shows how an inelastic

investment demand means that investment cannot be stimulated by interest rate changes. We can identify situations in which policy will be powerful or weak by playing around with the parameters.

The task is simple. The student confirms that the liquidity trap can be applied to a random economy. For any parameter set, perfectly elastic money demand makes the money supply powerless.

3D. Deriving AD: The final screencast derives AD by varying P and tracking Y_e. The *ISLMAD* sheet separates the money supply and the price level. Changing P changes real balances and shifts LM, producing a new equilibrium level of output. The sheet shows an AD curve under the ISLM chart. The screencast explains that AD is not a giant micro demand curve and stresses this key point at the end. Instead, AD is an equilibrium set of points, just like IS and LM. The exogenous variable is P, so it shifts left and right (and points off the AD curve are attracted in a horizontal fashion). The screencast concludes by exploring how policy tools shift AD. Unlike G and T, which shift AD by a constant amount no matter the price level, the magnitude of a money supply shock depends on the price level.

The task is difficult. The student must determine if changes in the MPC shift AD by a constant amount like G and T or a varying amount like the money supply. This conceptually challenging question is hard to see on the graph with small changes in the MPC. Changing the MPC to 0.1 makes it clear that the MPC, like the money supply, shifts AD by more as the price level falls. The mathematics behind the result are that equilibrium Y is a linear function of G and T (see the *Math* sheet), but the derivative of Y_e with respect to M^s includes a P term, and Y_e is a nonlinear function of the MPC.

Conclusion

The *ISLM.xls* workbook is rather complicated and requires patient attention to detail. Unlike a conventional textbook, whose lack of explicit, concrete functional relationships gives license to draw and say anything, the Excel implementation of the ISLM Model imposes tight constraints. There is a return, however, in that the properties of the model can be displayed and questions answered with no ambiguity or hand waving.

Veteran professors may disagree with some of the pedagogical decisions made, such as using the no-feedback version of the ISLM Model before deriving the IS and LM curves or the emphasis placed or proper shifting of curves. One of the tremendous advantages of these workbooks, however, is that nothing is set in stone. You are free to manipulate, reorganize, and recast the material to suit your own tastes and preferences.

The venerable ISLM Model can convey Keynesian ideas and appropriately challenges students to work hard to master the model. Once the mechanics are understood, the model offers a window through which to interpret news events and alternative policies. The *Final* sheet in the workbook summarizes important ideas and paves the way for the final version of the Keynesian model included in these materials.

Sources and Further Reading

The epigraph is from O. Blanchard, "What Do We Know about Macroeconomics That Fisher and Wicksell Did Not?," *Quarterly Journal of Economics* 115, no. 4 (2000): 1405, http://www.jstor.org/stable/2586928.

5.5

The ISLMADAS Model: *ISLMADAS.xls*

Whether the IS-LM framework is to be vilified for its
elusive, chameleon-like character or to be cherished for its
flexibility remains an open question.
– Sandy Darity and Warren Young

Quick Summary

To access *ISLMADAS.xls*, visit

http://www.depauw.edu/learn/macroexcel/excelworkbooks/ISLMModel/
ISLMADAS.xls

ISLMADAS.xls augments the ISLM Model with ADAS. The feedback mechanism from P to real balances and the mechanics of the model are emphasized, with continuing exploration of comparative statics properties and multipliers. Short- and long-run equilibration are reviewed, and the Lucas critique is demonstrated.

Screencasts

- http://vimeo.com/econexcel/islmadasintro: introduces the ISLMADAS Model and points out how it extends the ISLM Model by endogenizing the price level; this is similar to the way that ISLM extended the simple Keynesian Cross graph by connecting income to money demand
- http://vimeo.com/econexcel/islmadasadjustment: shows how the ISLMADAS Model determines short- and long-run equilibrium positions for the economy
- http://vimeo.com/econexcel/islmadasmultiplier: shows how the price feedback in the ISLMADAS model shrinks the G multiplier relative to the ISLM Model, where there is no price feedback
- http://vimeo.com/econexcel/islmadasart: shows how to draw the ISLMADAS Model "by hand" and explains how the IS and LM curves adjust to the ADAS graph

- http://vimeo.com/econexcel/islmadasapplied: shows how to use the ISLMADAS Model to interpret shocks and apply policies
- http://vimeo.com/econexcel/islmadaslucas: explains how the Lucas critique applies to the ISLMADAS Model – by shifting SRAS as policies are enacted to stimulate the economy, rational agents short-circuit the policy maker's attempts to manipulate the economy; policy is best understood as game theory, not as turning dials to control a machine

Introduction

The *ISLMADAS.xls* workbook presents the ISLMADAS Model as a natural extension of the ISLM Model. Having derived AD as $Y_e = f(P)$, short-run (SRAS) and long-run (LRAS) aggregate supply are added to enable determination of equilibrium P and Y. As with the ISLM Model, the emphasis is on understanding the linkages among graphs and variables, how the model behaves under different parameter values and elasticities, and how to use the model to interpret events of the day and policy effects.

Common Problems for Students

While individual details can cause problems, the real difficulty in the ISLMADAS Model lies in its seemingly overwhelming number of variables and intricate relationships between graphs. Economics students are used to one graph (e.g., supply and demand), and two-graph displays are much less common (e.g., total costs stacked above marginal and average cost curves). The ISLMADAS apparatus is much more complicated than anything they have seen before.

Getting all of the pieces exactly right and learning how a shock propagates to shift or move along a curve in each graph in the model is hard work. Excel does offer a tremendous advantage in this respect, since it can update graphs instantly after a parameter change. By practicing and playing with the workbook, students can eventually master the model.

A helpful tip to emphasize repeatedly is that the best way to use the model is to start at the end, the ADAS graph, and work your way back to the other graphs. This sort of backward induction is not intuitively obvious to most students. They assume, for example, that an analysis of an increase in G should begin at the beginning, with the goods market. The problem with this strategy is that PE is going to bounce all over the place as income and price feedback mechanisms impact the goods market. Explaining to students that the ADAS graph reveals the "final answer" because AD has goods and money market equilibrium baked into it goes a long way toward helping students understand how the model works.

Another helpful teaching tip is to be clear about how P feeds into the money market through real balances, M^s/P. It makes sense to take advantage of the intellectual capital accumulated in the ISLM Model, where Y fed back into money demand to produce interest rate changes and eventually affected Y. In a similar fashion, when we endogenize P, anything that moves the price level will affect real balances and propagate to the goods market through investment.

Comparing Figures 5.4.1 and 5.5.1 (which can be done in the *ISLMADAS.xls* file by comparing the *NoPFeedback* and *ISLMADAS* sheets) is one way to drive this point home. By carefully examining and listing the properties of the two displays, the implications of endogenizing P can be understood.

Finally, although advantageous in terms of a single handout or slide, suppression of all of the graphs, except ADAS, is quite dangerous. Keeping the full model on display (as done in the Excel workbook and Figure 5.5.1) reminds the student of the entire model and the intricate relationships connecting the parameters and producing the general equilibrium solution.

The ISLMADAS Model

As usual, the *Intro* sheet lays out the primary ideas. It explains how the ADAS component was added on to the ISLM Model, producing a general equilibrium system with three endogenous variables, and offers a history of economic thought lesson on the development of the model. The sheet prints on six landscaped pages for convenient use as a handout during a class lecture or for a reading assignment:

Model Equations:
$C = C_0 + C_1(Y - T)$ where $0 < C_1 < 1$
$I = I_0 + I_1 r$ $I_1 < 0$
$G = G$
$PE = C + I + G$
$L = L_0 + L_r r + L_Y Y$
  where $L_r < 0$ and $L_Y \geq 0$
$M^s = \frac{M}{P}$
Equilibrium Conditions:
$Y = PE$
$L = M^s$

The ISLM Model to the left produces an AD curve.
We add an AS relationship:
$P = P^e + \alpha(Y - Y^F)$
Equilibrium Condition:
$AD = AS$

As was the case with the *ISLM.xls* workbook, a hidden *Math* sheet can be revealed by a button click from the *ISLMADAS* sheet (near cell K1) to display the step-by-step algebraic solution. With P in the denominator of real balances, the quadratic formula must be used to solve for the intersection of AD and AS. The *Math* sheet explains this in detail.

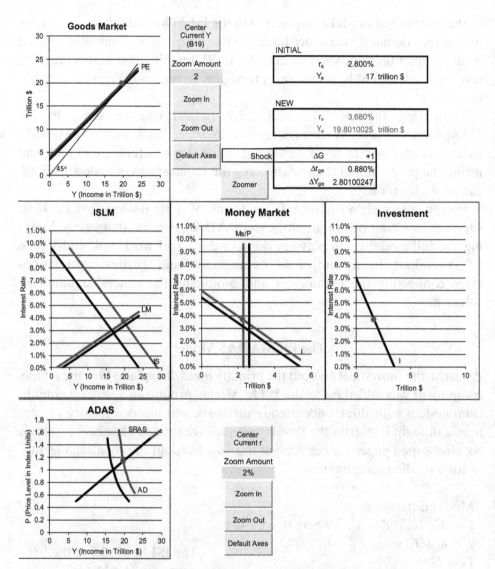

Figure 5.5.1. An increase in *G* in the ISLMADAS Model.
Source: ISLMADAS sheet in *ISLMADAS.xls.*

The same teaching strategy used previously is adopted in that the fixed-price ISLM Model is an ISLMADAS Model with a horizontal AS curve. This serves as the starting point from which the conventional ISLMADAS with an upward sloping SRAS curve is the next logical step. This makes clear the connection between the two models and conveys the notion of a progression of models from simple Keynesian Cross to ISLM and now ISLMADAS.

The workbook makes no mention of a particular AS story. Thus, this implementation of the model works with any textbook. As Mankiw (2013, 416) points out, it does not matter how the upward sloping AS curve is motivated, as long as it is a variant of the familiar $P = P^e + \alpha(Y - Y^F)$. The Excel implementation uses expected price to shift SRAS if output is off its long-run equilibrium position.

No mention of this is made in the screencast, but it is true that the model presents different levels of policy difficulty depending on the type of shock. A decrease in AD is easily remedied by appropriate stimulus, while a decrease in AS presents a dilemma because policy makers must choose between unemployment and inflation. For professors interested in presenting the Phillips Curve, exploring stagflation as a decrease in the AS curve is a natural jumping-off point.

The *Intro* sheet presents three criticisms of the model (mentioned in the introduction to this chapter), but the most serious problem has to do with the very core of what it means to be Keynesian. The addition of LRAS makes the model automatically stabilizing, and that, it would seem, is quite un-Keynesian. Time permitting, a class discussion on what it means to be Keynesian would be worthwhile. There may not be an exact answer here, but a conversation on what characteristics contribute to a Keynesian perspective would help students understand the model and how Keynes changed macroeconomics.

Screencasts and Tasks

1. Introducing the ISLMADAS Model: The first screencast begins by pointing out that Excel may have trouble with a user-defined function, ISLMADAS(), which provides the analytical solution to the model. The solution is to press the F9 key to recalculate the workbook. The instructions for using this function are discussed later in the video. The bottom line is that entering a formula for this version of the model is too cumbersome because we need to use the quadratic formula and because the reduced-form solution contains so many parameters that the formula would be difficult to read. The *Math* sheet is briefly displayed so the viewer can see how the solution is found by equating AS and AD (which are derived from IS and LM). The ISLMADAS() function code is accessible in Visual Basic.

   The screencast proceeds by explaining that several aggregate supply stories are consistent with an upward sloping SRAS curve. It then discusses how we have endogenized P and that the ADAS graph contains the final answer. To convey the idea of a progression of models, the *NoPFeedback* sheet is used. With a zero slope, AS is horizontal and the model collapses back into the previous, fixed-price ISLM Model. By changing the money supply and comparing the horizontal versus the upward sloping AS cases, it is easy to see that the upward sloping AS version behaves differently. The price level rises when AD shifts right, and the increase in equilibrium Y is not as great compared to the horizontal AS case. To continue pushing the idea of a progression of models, the screencast sets $L_Y = 0$ in the *NoPFeedback* sheet and shows how this produces a horizontal LM curve. The student can see how we have progressed from the initial Keynesian Cross diagram to ISLM and now we are in ISLMADAS. This strong visual explanation is a good way to explain the models. The end of the video reminds the viewer that AS and AD do not work like micro supply and demand curves. The intersection pins down the final answer, but it does not equilibrate by shortages and surpluses pushing price to equilibrium.

The task asks the student to explain the how the price feedback mechanism affects the model by applying an AS slope of 0.1 to a randomly generated economy from the *NoPFeedback* sheet. Excel will display the zero AS slope as the base case, and when the student changes the AS slope, SRAS will be shown as a red, upward sloping line. This gives the student a way to answer the question by comparing how the model behaves differently with horizontal versus upward sloping SRAS. The next screencast reviews the answer to this task.

2. Adjustment in the ISLMADAS Model: After briefly reviewing the implications of an upward sloping SRAS, this screencast focuses on how the model will adjust in the long run to its LRAS value. The example used is a negative shock to the investment intercept. By drawing a simple stylized graph of a growth path, the screencast explains how this short-run model fits into a long-run setting. It is a static model, a single frame in a moving picture. The video raises the issue of whether this model deserves to be called a Keynesian model if it has forces that bring it to full-employment equilibrium. In terms of long-run adjustment, the variable that shifts the SRAS over time is the expected price level. By clicking the [Chase P] button, the expected price parameter chases equilibrium price and drives Y to its long-run value. The screencast points out that the speed of adjustment depends on how expectations are formed. The viewer is encouraged to search the Web to learn more about adaptive versus rational expectations. By way of conclusion, it is noted that we do not typically see deflation as predicted by the model because policy makers do not stand by and allow the system to stabilize on its own.

The task is a straightforward application of the screencast. The student draws a random economy and explains how it will reach its long-run equilibrium. By construction, $Y_e < Y_f$, so the answer must show SRAS shifting right as expected price chases the equilibrium price level.

3. Multiplier Attenuation in the ISLMADAS Model: From the *NoPFeedback* sheet, we see that the G multiplier is 3.33 and that it was 5 in the simple Keynesian Cross model, so it shrunk when we added the income feedback to money demand. To show that the G multiplier gets even smaller when we endogenize P in the ISLMADAS Model, the ISLM and ADAS graphs are copied and pasted as images. These charts have a transparent background, so it is easy to compare the horizontal versus upward sloping SRAS cases. By looking carefully at the ADAS graph, we can see that the upward sloping SRAS graph produces a lower level of equilibrium Y. The ISLM graph is another way to explain why the multiplier is smaller – LM shifts up as P rises, and this produces a smaller change in equilibrium Y.

The task is challenging because the student must extend the qualitative idea that a nonzero SRAS slope attenuates the G multiplier to the quantitative idea that the greater the slope, the more the multiplier is reduced. By following the chart copy-and-paste strategy, it can be demonstrated that the steeper the slope of SRAS, the higher is P_e and the lower is Y_e, given an increase in G, ceteris paribus.

4. The Art of the ISLMADAS Model: This screencast presents the model in a more traditional, abstract way. It uses a series of drawing objects in the *Art* sheet (which is revealed by clicking the [Show Art] button from the *ISLMADAS* sheet) to build the model from the ground up. A running commentary provides information to help the student understand the IS, LM, AD, SRAS, and LRAS functions. The screencast goes on to show how an increase in G is analyzed by first shifting AD, then forcing the IS and LM curves to conform to the ADAS graph. It stresses that because P increased, you have to shift LM up.

   The task asks the student to do the same analysis as the screencast, except for a decrease in G. The answers to this question and to several other shocks are available by scrolling far right in the *Art* sheet. As with other workbooks, worries about students discovering this resource can be alleviated by deleting the charts. With no reason to scroll right, however, it is unlikely that a student will stumble upon this material.

5. How to Use the ISLMADAS Model: This screencast demonstrates how the ISLMADAS Model can be used to interpret real-world events and policies. There are two basic approaches: (1) from a recession, policy moves can be evaluated, and (2) starting from long-run equilibrium, stories about the economy can be incorporated. The former approach is shown with fiscal and money multipliers. Money demand is then made very interest rate elastic, and it is clear that the money supply solution that worked so well before is doing almost nothing to stimulate an almost vertical AD. This is because the money supply has almost no effect on the interest rate and, therefore, investment is almost unchanged. To illustrate the second approach, a collapse in housing prices is interpreted as a decrease in the consumption intercept. The screencast also mentions how rising oil prices in the 1970s produced stagflation, which can be modeled as a decrease in SRAS.

   There are two tasks associated with this screencast. The first asks the student to explore the effect of extremely inelastic investment demand in a randomly generated economy. Of course, such a scenario would leave the Fed powerless because changes in the interest rate will not affect investment or equilibrium output.

   The second task points out that we have not seen prices fall during recent recessions but invites the student to find data on the price level during the Great Depression. The deflation predicted by the ISLMADAS Model conforms closely to what happened during this crisis.

   The *Course Materials* page at http://www.depauw.edu/learn/macroexcel has instructions for student presentations from a list of historical episodes: the Panic of 1907, the Great Depression, the recession of 1953, the Kennedy tax cut, OPEC stagflation, the monetarist experiment, the dot-com recession, and the Great Recession. Students research the episode then explain how the ISLMADAS Model can be used to interpret and understand what happened.

6. The Lucas Critique: The final screencast offers criticisms of the Keynesian Model. It begins by pointing out that we simply do not have the necessary information about parameter values to use the model. Along the same lines, the model is nowhere near complete. We do not have an international sector or exchange rates, and those are serious shortcomings. We also do not know how long policies take to work and the economy itself is a moving target. The screencast then turns to the Lucas critique and elevates it above these other criticisms. It describes how Lucas argued that the economy is not a machine and that when you apply a policy, the agents in the system react to it, thereby changing the structural parameters of the model.

The task is quite open ended. It sends the student to the Fed's website to search for a news release or policy statement that reflects the Lucas critique. This assignment has the virtue of having the student explore the Fed's rich resources, while connecting the model to the important issues of the day. It is not difficult to find language in a Fed press release or paper that reflects an understanding of policy as game theory.

Conclusion

The four workbooks that comprise the Keynesian Model contain a great deal of information and require a substantial time commitment. The advantages for student learning are varied, but perhaps none is more important that the ability of a student to intelligently process current events. Gärtner et al. (2013) surveyed undergraduate macro professors after the most recent financial crises and found little change in the models used in courses. This may reflect inertia, but a master of the ISLM and ISLMADAS models would have no problem interpreting the Great Recession and resulting policy moves in an undergraduate lecture. This, in a nutshell, is why the ISLM and ADAS models survive in the undergraduate curriculum.

There are, of course, a variety of ways to extend the model. Smaller tweaks would include modeling taxes as tY instead of simply as T or making consumption a function of the interest rate or price level. Connecting changes in output to price inflation to produce a Phillips Curve relationship or creating an Okun's Law graph with changes in unemployment and growth in GDP are other ways to include more content. More substantial extensions would include adding an international sector to create a Mundell–Fleming Model. These would be excellent projects for an independent study or advanced undergraduate courses.

ISLM and its progeny will forever be attacked by some as ad hoc and lacking rigor. Others are sure there is nothing Keynesian in these models and a gross fraud has been perpetrated. The greatest threat to ISLM is the lack of training in graduate programs. But until someone figures out how to deliver a micro-founded, real business cycle, or dynamic stochastic general equilibrium model in a way digestible by undergraduates, ISLM will live on.

Sources and Further Reading

The epigraph is from W. Darity Jr. and W. Young, "IS-LM: An Inquest," *History of Political Economy* 27, no. 1 (1995): 1, http://muse.jhu.edu/journals/history_of_political_economy/summary/v032/32.2vroey.html.

Gärtner, M., B. Griesbach, and F. Junga. 2013. "Teaching Macroeconomics after the Crisis: A Survey among Undergraduate Instructors in Europe and the United States." *Journal of Economic Education* 44, no. 4: 406–16. http://www.tandfonline.com/doi/abs/10.1080/00220485.2013.827050.

Mankiw, N. 2013. *Macroeconomics*. 9th ed. Worth.

6

Epilogue

> Exceptional teachers treat their lectures, discussion
> sections, problem-based sessions, and other elements of
> teaching as serious intellectual endeavors as intellectually
> demanding and important as their research
> and scholarship.
> – Ken Bain

The idea driving this book was simple: to share content that has been successful in teaching macroeconomics. The goal was to enable a professor to quickly and easily incorporate these materials into a course. This epilogue is designed to lower any barriers even further, offering a handy overview of all files and specific Excel skills, along with suggestions for utilizing the workbooks and screencasts. As mentioned previously, please visit the *Course Materials* section of http://www.depauw.edu/learn/macroexcel for a course syllabus and full set of daily handouts for an undergraduate macro course.

Figure 6.1 shows how the workbooks are organized into five independent topics. This can be used as a guide to curricular planning by matching each topic to a syllabus or table of contents from a favorite textbook. Visit http://www.depauw.edu/learn/macroexcel/screencasts for a listing of each screencast in each workbook.

Figure 6.2 provides a different perspective, listing the workbooks that use an advanced, specific Excel skill. These workbooks are quite general and can be used in a wide range of courses beyond macroeconomics. You can sprinkle a single workbook and screencast into any course to add the variation in delivery that reenergizes the classroom and boosts student learning.

These materials are modular, and you can choose to use, for example, only the *FRED* add-in workbooks or only a single workbook, but they provide an even higher level of flexibility beyond the ability to pick and choose specific pieces. These workbooks are not like a printed book in that you can take ownership and modify them as you wish. This is an incredibly powerful aspect

Charting	Economic Growth	Solow Model	Data	Keynesian Model
HowToChart.xls RecessionChart.xls	MaddisonData.xls	KAcc.xls GoldenRule.xls Population.xls TechProgress.xls	GDP.xls Unem.xls Inflation.xls Money.xls	KCross.xls MoneyMarket.xls ISLM.xls ISLMADAS.xls
Add-ins:				
EconChart.xla			Fred_2013.xlam	ScenCS.xla

Figure 6.1. An overview of all Excel files. All workbooks freely available from http://www.depauw.edu/learn/macroexcel.

Excel Workbook	Advanced, Specific Excel Skill
HowToChart.xls Population.xls	Directly edit SERIES formula in a chart
RecessionChart.xls	Add shaded bars for recessions (or other variable)
RecessionChart.xls	How to install an add-in (EconChart.xla)
MaddisonData.xls	How to use Equation Editor
MaddisonData.xls	Using Excel's RANK function
GoldenRule.xls Unem.xls KCross.xls MoneyMarket.xls	Using Excel's Solver to find an optimal solution
Population.xls Unem.xls	Using Excel's PivotTable
Population.xls	Working with scenarios and Scenario Manager
Population.xls	Using Excel's MATCH function
TechProgress.xls Unem.xls	Incorporating randomness and Monte Carlo simulation
Unem.xls	Using an array function to randomly sample from a list
Money.xls	Using Zoomer tool in EconChart add-in
Money.xls	Using the Hodrick-Prescott (HP) array function
MoneyMarket.xls	Working with Scenario Comparative Statics (ScenCS.xla)
GDP.xls Unem.xls Inflation.xls Money.xls	FRED add-in (including searching and data manipulation)

Figure 6.2. A list of Excel skills.

of teaching with these Excel files. The take-home message is to be proactive and treat the workbooks as adaptable. Nothing is set in stone.

Successful teaching depends on experimentation, change, and mixing modes of delivery. Unfortunately, having given a number of presentations and workshops over the years (visit http://www.depauw.edu/learn/econexcel), I recognize that many professors are not risk takers or trailblazers. The inertia, once a syllabus or textbook has been chosen, is quite high. Faculty follow the textbook sequentially, skipping a chapter here or there. Like with smartphone providers and hair stylists, once chosen, we stay faithful to the same text for years, with small tweaks to the syllabus. To optimize use of these files, this approach has to change in a big way.

Consider the textbook choice problem, perhaps for a course taught for the first time. The professor picks a text after a complicated weighing of various factors. While text A does one thing well, it fails at another, and text B manages to be decent at most things. Text C uses too much math, and text D's graphics are eye-catching but the low level of theory is a deal breaker. Whether and how much price matters is another issue entirely, but eventually the professor chooses a text, often settling on the least offensive option. A key point is that the textbook is a finished product, with no potential for modification. The text, graphs, and examples are frozen.

Unlike a standard, printed textbook, these Excel workbooks are completely yours to modify as needed. You do not have to accept the workbook as is. Move a chart if you don't like it. Change the color or formatting. Add a chart or cell. Right-click a button or scroll bar to select it, then cut or drag it somewhere else. Hide a sheet or add a sheet with your own material. You are absolutely free and empowered to alter or extend a workbook however you wish. Some content looks cluttered or truncated on smaller screens but beautiful on a large screen. Then arrange the objects and cells as you wish and save as to a new workbook, for example, *xxxSmallDisplay.xls*.

In a workshop, someone once told me that he was scared that he would break something, but that fear is unfounded because you can always download an original version of the workbook again. Alternatively, copy the sheet and then modify it.

The power at your disposal extends to the text in the Excel workbooks. The *Intro* sheets in the Keynesian Model workbooks, for example, are designed to be printed. You may edit and change these sheets to your liking. Add whatever you think has been overlooked that is crucial and delete anything you think is wrong. Highlight text or add graphics. These materials are not a finished work that must be used as is, a painting to be hung on the wall. Instead, they are clay – easily transformed and augmented. To optimally use these files, explore and be bold. Modify. Create.

The more you personalize these materials and incorporate yourself into the workbooks, the more successful and productive your teaching will be.

Likewise, the more stories you tell (about yourself and the history of models, variables, and economists) and the more you connect the content to something tangible, the more your students will learn.

It is certainly easier and lower cost to pick a textbook and assign chapters to weeks on a syllabus, with chalk and talk each class and multiple-choice exams. If, however, you are looking for deeper understanding by your students, using of any of these Excel workbooks will signal the value you attach to your teaching. It undoubtedly will take additional effort and time to master these new ways of presenting content, but if my personal experience is any guide, it will be worth the cost.

Sources and Further Reading

The epigraph is from Ken Bain's *What the Best College Teachers Do* (Harvard University Press, 2004), 17. Bain identifies best practices, attitudes, and methods of successful college teachers.

Printed in the United States
by Baker & Taylor Publisher Services.

Printed in the United States
by Baker & Taylor Publisher Services